When Cities Lobby

When Cities Lobby

*How Local Governments Compete for
Power in State Politics*

JULIA PAYSON

OXFORD
UNIVERSITY PRESS

OXFORD
UNIVERSITY PRESS

Oxford University Press is a department of the University of Oxford. It furthers
the University's objective of excellence in research, scholarship, and education
by publishing worldwide. Oxford is a registered trade mark of Oxford University
Press in the UK and certain other countries.

Published in the United States of America by Oxford University Press
198 Madison Avenue, New York, NY 10016, United States of America.

Library of Congress Cataloging-in-Publication Data
Names: Payson, Julia, author.
Title: When cities lobby : how local governments compete for
power in state politics / Julia Payson.
Description: New York, NY : Oxford University Press, [2022] |
Includes bibliographical references and index.
Identifiers: LCCN 2021038643 (print) | LCCN 2021038644 (ebook) |
ISBN 9780197615263 (hardback) | ISBN 9780197615270 (paperback) |
ISBN 9780197615294 (epub)
Subjects: LCSH: Lobbying—United States. | Local government—United States. |
Polarization (Social sciences)—United States.
Classification: LCC JK1118 .P39 2022 (print) | LCC JK1118 (ebook) |
DDC 324/.40973—dc23/eng/20211001
LC record available at https://lccn.loc.gov/2021038643
LC ebook record available at https://lccn.loc.gov/2021038644

DOI: 10.1093/oso/9780197615263.001.0001

1 3 5 7 9 8 6 4 2

Paperback printed by LSC communications, United States of America
Hardback printed by Bridgeport National Bindery, Inc., United States of America

For Mom

Contents

Online replication materials for this book are deposited in the Harvard Dataverse (https://dataverse.harvard.edu/).

Figures

Acknowledgments

I'm deeply grateful for the people who helped inspire this book. My first thanks go to Terry Moe, my advisor at Stanford. Terry is one of the most brilliant political scientists, clear thinkers, beautiful writers, and supportive mentors that I've ever met. He always encouraged me to pursue research I genuinely cared about and was a champion of this project from the beginning. I am also indebted to each of my dissertation committee members at Stanford: Bruce Cain, Clayton Nall, and Andy Hall. Bruce introduced me to lobbyists and state lawmakers in California who provided invaluable insight about how city lobbying actually worked. He always reminded me that my research mattered, and I'm so proud to join the ranks of his vast and impressive network of former students. Clayton constantly pushed me to develop my ideas into clear and tractable arguments, and he helped me to frame my research in terms of well-defined questions and a coherent political story. To this day, I still draw inspiration from my time as a teaching assistant for his Urban Politics class at Stanford. Finally, Andy will always set the standard for me of what it means to be a careful and principled empirical researcher. He makes political science a better discipline in every way, and I'm so grateful for his mentorship and friendship.

This book wouldn't have been possible without the keen insights of the many state and local officials and city advocates who were generous enough to speak with me over the course of the project. Thank you especially to Jason and Anthony Gonsalves, Jennifer Abele, Ron Book, Dana Fenton, Chris McKenzie, Yiaway Yeh, Conan Smith, Amy Paulin, Kirk Profit, Shelley Mayer, and Anthony Santos—I'm grateful for your time and public service. Over the past year, I've also deeply appreciated the advice and enthusiasm of my stellar editor, Dave McBride. The anonymous reviewers who read the manuscript provided constructive and thoughtful suggestions, and the entire team at Oxford University Press has been fantastic to work with. Finally, I am thankful for the capable research assistance of the many RAs who helped me collect data for this project—especially Matthew Brigstock, who also read early drafts of several chapters.

Back when this research was just shaping up as a dissertation project, I was extremely lucky to receive feedback and encouragement from many faculty members at Stanford. I especially want to thank Justin Grimmer, Mike Tomz, David Brady, and Shanto Iyengar for their help and support over the years. I'm also grateful for my colleagues in the Politics Department at New York University (NYU)—my current intellectual home and a vibrant scholarly community. I particularly want to acknowledge Dimitri Landa, Cathy Hafer, Sanford Gordon, Hye Young You, and Becky Morton for attending a chapter workshop that fundamentally reshaped the manuscript and helped move this work from dissertation to book. Becky: we miss you. Patrick Egan also attended the workshop and read multiple versions of my prospectus, and he is among the kindest, sharpest, most generous, and most politically astute colleagues I have ever met. Jonathan Nagler similarly read multiple drafts of the book prospectus and has taught me a great deal as a co-author, mentor, and fellow jazz enthusiast. David Stasavage has always provided sage advice and served as an exemplary advocate for junior faculty members in the department. Finally, thank you to the staff of the Politics Department who keep everything running smoothly—especially Kim Borden and Stephanie Nica—and to Sandy Gordon for his work and support as department chair.

I am filled with gratitude for everyone else at NYU Politics who has made New York feel like home both intellectually and socially, including Amy Catalinac, Arthur Spirling, Pablo Querubín, Arturas Rozenas, Melissa Schwartzberg, Chris Dawes, and Alejandro Velasco. I especially want to thank Gwyneth McClendon and Hye Young You, who joined the faculty at NYU at the same time as I did and are two of the most brilliant and wonderful people, friends, and political scientists that I know.

A generous fellowship at the Center for the Study of Democratic Politics at Princeton University provided me with the time and resources I needed to complete the manuscript. Brandice Canes-Wrone provided extremely helpful scholarly and professional advice and was exceptional as the director of the fellows, and Michele Epstein was one of the most organized, kind, and effective administrators I have ever met. This research also benefited tremendously from a book talk organized by Jeff Jenkins at the 2021 Local Political Economy Symposium at University of Southern California (USC). I am indebted in so many ways to Liz Gerber, who carefully read the entire manuscript as well as earlier drafts of individual chapters and papers. Liz's research sparked my interest in local politics while I was still in graduate school, and her friendship, encouragement, and intellectual mentorship over the years have truly been a gift.

So many others have shaped my research and provided invaluable feedback at various stages of the project. In particular, I want to thank Jessica Trounstine, Nolan McCarty, Chris Warshaw, and especially Sarah Anzia—a fellow Terry Moe student and one of my academic role models. I also want to acknowledge Karen Halttunen and Mark Kann, two of my college professors at USC who inspired me to pursue a career in academia.

Beyond the many brilliant and thoughtful teachers and researchers who I've been lucky enough to learn from throughout my life, I'm also beyond grateful for the friends who have supported me along the way. Helen Moser, Lilly McKibbin, and Jennifer Allen were the best college roommates I could have asked for and have been my steadfast cheerleaders ever since. At Stanford, I can't imagine having survived my graduate work without the game nights, problem set parties, and Friday happy hours. Thank you especially to Darin Christensen, Francisco Garfias, Ramya Parthasarathy, Ashley Lagaron, Kirk Bansak, David Pena, Mathilde Emeriau, David Hausman, Emily Zhang, Jane Esberg, Dorothy Kronick, Kerry Persen, Adriane Fresh, Nick Eubank, Eric Min, and Dan Thompson. Jane Esberg also provided expert editing on the book's early chapters and has been a truly exceptional friend to me, both in California and now in New York.

I am also grateful to my family: Mom, Ali, John, Tutu, Pop, Dad, Babcia, and the many household cats (especially Stella, Nigel, Smokey, and Chums). Thank you for loving me and being proud of me and for your constant support. And to the people who became my family in the Bay Area: Dani Schumacher, John Fyffe, Sierra and Luis Villaran, Mark Donohue, Jason and Rebekah Walker, David Zhai, Avery Lindemen, Evan Dart, and Evan Lee (and now Maddy Dart and Naina Prasad!)—never forget how awesome we are. I love you all very much.

1

Cities as Lobbyists

When people think of pork-barrel spending and earmarks, people think of high-class lobbyists ... but the truth is, it's local governments who lobby for earmarks and government money.

—Vice President Leslie Paige,
Citizens Against Government Waste

The notion that our tax dollars are going to lobby for government, I bring that up to people and they are absolutely shocked by it. Government[s] in and of themselves are becoming special interests.

—Senator Owen Hill (R-Colorado Springs),
Colorado Springs Gazette

In 2017, a Gallup poll asked people to rate the "honesty and ethical standards" of various occupations. Respondents offered highly favorable assessments of nurses, teachers, and pharmacists. Lawyers and advertisers were viewed with more suspicion, ranking in the bottom third of the survey. The profession that came in dead last? Lobbyists—right behind used car salespeople and members of Congress.[1] When most Americans think of lobbyists, they imagine slick power brokers representing wealthy corporations and special interests. What many people may not know is that the towns and cities they live in also employ professional lobbyists. In fact, over 60 percent of US residents live in cities that have hired a lobbyist at some point to advocate for local interests at either the state or the federal level. And in some states, like California, local governments spend more money lobbying than any other interest group sector.

Governments of all types lobby each other frequently, both in the United States and in other federal systems. Intuitively, whenever one level of government has fiscal or administrative authority over another, the lower level will have incentives to try to shape the policy and funding decisions of the higher level through lobbying. At its most basic meaning, lobbying simply describes efforts by groups and individuals to influence government policy. In practice, however, lobbying has come to be associated with the paid activities of professional advocates. Local governments are no exception. Historically, most local advocacy efforts were organized directly by municipal boosters, businessmen, and city elites (Teaford 1984). But over the past few decades, local officials have increasingly come to rely on paid lobbyists to navigate the world of intergovernmental politics on their behalf.

Take Corcoran, a mid-sized city in Central California. For years, Corcoran officials tried unsuccessfully to obtain state funding to upgrade their aging police facilities. In 2014, the city council decided to take a more proactive approach. They hired a lobbying firm called CrisCom to work with their state assembly member to secure state money for the project. When Governor Jerry Brown signed the budget into law the following year, Corcoran ended up receiving several million dollars in earmarked funds that allowed them to begin construction on a new police station. Corcoran officials later thanked their State Assembly Member Rudy Salas (D-Bakersfield) for advocating diligently on their behalf in Sacramento. But the city's police chief also singled out CrisCom, saying the lobbyists deserved "a lot of credit" for the outcome.[2]

The neighboring city of Hanford wasn't so lucky. Hanford officials had used CrisCom to represent them in the past, but the city council voted to terminate the city's lobbying contract by a 3–2 vote in early 2014. While the police department urged the city to continue their lobbying efforts, several council members expressed frustration that the process was taking so long and questioned whether paying for lobbying services was a good investment of city funds. Hanford ultimately failed to secure any of the subsequent budgetary windfall, despite sitting in the same legislative district as Corcoran.

This story raises a variety of questions that touch on the themes that run throughout this book. When and why do some local officials choose to hire lobbyists to represent them in other levels of government? How does this ability to pay for representation influence politics and policymaking? And what are the broader implications for intergovernmental representation? Marshaling original quantitative and qualitative evidence from dozens of sources—including newly compiled longitudinal data on lobbying disclosures in all fifty states—the following chapters offer new insight into what happens when local officials hire lobbyists to compete for power in the United States.

Specifically, I focus on the lobbying behavior of municipalities targeting their state governments. Across the country, nearly 20,000 cities, towns, and villages annually raise over half a trillion dollars in revenue to provide essential public services. Over 80 percent of the US population lives within the boundaries of an incorporated municipality, and municipal officials make crucial decisions in areas ranging from education and public safety to affordable housing, transportation, and environmental sustainability. Throughout the book, I'll follow the US Census Bureau and use the terms *city* and *municipality* interchangeably to refer to "political subdivisions within which a municipal corporation has been established to provide general local government for a specific population in a defined area."[3] According to this definition, cities don't only include major metropolitan centers like New York, San Francisco, and Chicago. While I often break down my analyses by city size in order to explore how lobbying dynamics vary across large and small communities, one of the goals of this project is to generalize as much as possible about the conditions under which *all* cities lobby—not just urban centers.

Regardless of size, cities share the important trait of being legal entities created by their state governments. As a result, states shape and constrain the decisions available to local officials in important ways. In the nineteenth and early twentieth century, state legislators actively approved, amended, and revoked the charters that defined the powers and organizational structure available to their municipal governments (Beard 1913; Allard, Burns, and Gamm 1998). More recently, states have flexed their constitutional authority by engaging in preemption efforts aimed at limiting cities' ability to pass local ordinances on policies ranging from minimum wage to paid family leave to gun control. Of course, federal policies can impact cities as well. Big-city mayors have periodically sought to influence national politics, especially during the New Deal Era (Haider 1974; Ogorzalek 2018). But cities are first and foremost creatures of the state, which means that the actions of state governments tend to be particularly consequential at the local level.

City officials don't sit back passively and hope for favorable treatment. Instead, cities jostle for influence over the state policies that affect them through lobbying. Local leaders often describe their lobbyists as being essential to the process of navigating increasingly complex state policy environments. It turns out that this is especially true for large, urban areas that have been historically disadvantaged in state politics due to their numeric underrepresentation in state legislatures. However, I also discover that municipalities of all sizes experiment with lobbying to achieve a variety of goals—from securing additional grant money to coordinating communication across legislators to monitoring state actions. What determines when local officials take the costly step of hiring a lobbyist, and what do they get as a result?

One of the key theoretical insights of this book is that cities can use lobbyists to bridge the representational gaps that sometimes emerge as a result of their political geography. Compared to most other interest groups, cities are uniquely dependent on the state officials who are elected to represent them. Local governments enjoy a certain level of de facto representation by virtue of sitting in state and federal legislative districts that serve the same constituents. Elected officials in higher office are tasked with advocating for the local interests of their district, and they spend a great deal of time working to secure pork and policy benefits for their local governments. But as I describe in detail in Chapter 3, the quality of this vertical representation can vary dramatically. When communities struggle to secure funding and favorable policies directly from their elected delegation, they can purchase lobbyist representation to pursue other avenues of influence.

I uncover a variety of evidence consistent with this theoretical perspective. The places that are the most active lobbyists are precisely those that face uphill battles in achieving equal representation. These cities include urban metro areas that have suffered from historical malapportionment because of the way state legislative districts are drawn, as well as municipalities of all sizes whose districts elect legislators from the opposite political party. Lobbying is also particularly common in states with both professionalized state legislatures and term limits—conditions that make it difficult for local officials to develop strong relationships with their elected delegations.

But while intergovernmental advocacy can facilitate communication between state and local officials and serve as a useful complement to formal channels of representation, there are also potential downsides. Depending on which local governments take advantage of the opportunity to hire lobbyists and how effective their efforts are, lobbying might shift the policy-making process toward the interests of certain types of communities over others. In the world of interest group politics, we know that the priorities of larger, wealthier organizations tend to dominate. These groups are more likely to get involved in politics, and public policy more often aligns with their preferences (Mills 1956; Schattschneider 1960; Bartels 2008; Gilens 2012). I find that similar dynamics are at play when it comes to the lobbying efforts of municipal governments. Although more affluent localities don't actually hire lobbyists at higher rates than other cities, they are particularly adept at securing state funding when they do.

In other words, paying for lobbyist representation appears to be a double-edged sword for cities. Lobbying is an essential tool for local leaders seeking to amplify their voices in the complicated and often hostile world of state politics. The cities that are most likely to hire lobbyists are large urban centers that have long been underrepresented in our federal system—and, increasingly, blue-leaning cities engaged in preemption battles against Republican-led legislatures. But once we open the door to lobbying by these cities, localities of all types can deploy the same tactics, including high-income communities that may already enjoy substantial political and economic advantages.

These normative concerns echo a long-standing debate about the role of organized interests in democratic societies. Optimists emphasize the importance of information transfer for policymaking and consider lobbying to be a natural and healthy component of the linkage between citizens and elected officials (e.g., Truman 1951; Dahl 1961). Skeptics warn that differential access to resources and barriers to mobilization will lead to a system biased in favor of a few small, powerful groups with significant stakes in policy outcomes (e.g., Schattschneider 1960; Schlozman 1984). The goal of this book is not to convince you that city lobbying is inherently good or bad. Instead, it's to highlight the trade-offs that exist when local officials choose to pay for representation and to illustrate the range of consequences for cities, state policymakers, and the general public.

Throughout the book, I rely on lobbying disclosure filings to document how cities try to influence state policy. I discuss these data in detail in Chapter 2. A well-developed body of research on interest group politics tackles the question of whether lobbying is primarily about vote buying (Wright 1990; Mitchell and Munger 1991), access and information transfer (Austen-Smith 1993; Ansolabehere, De Figueiredo, and Snyder 2003), or legislative subsidy (Hall and Deardorff 2006). Scholars have studied bureaucratic lobbying (Gordon and Hafer 2005), debated the source of lobbyists' power (Blanes i Vidal, Draca, and Fons-Rosen 2012; Bertrand, Bombardini, and Trebbi 2014), estimated the returns to lobbying for organizations (De Figueiredo and Silverman 2006; Richter, Samphantharak, and Timmons 2009), and performed detailed case studies about the role of lobbying in shaping public policy (Truman 1951; Baumgartner et al. 2012).

The following chapters contribute to this literature by offering several insights into the lobbying process. Local governments are generally subject to open-meeting laws that require them to conduct their business in a publicly accessible manner. As a result, they are often more transparent about their lobbying goals than many other organizations. Municipalities also make a fantastic test bed to learn about the effects of lobbying because state transfers provide a clear, comparable way to measure what local officials get when they hire lobbyists. But the overall goal of this book is not to offer a new theory of lobbying per se. Instead, it is to advance our understanding of how cities shape the intergovernmental context in which they operate, and lobbying is an important part of the story.

To help me tell this story, I periodically draw from the voices of several experts that I spoke to over the course of my research. Anthony Gonsalves and his son Jason took over the family lobbying business founded by Joe Gonsalves in the 1970s, and they now advocate on behalf of dozens of small and mid-sized cities in California. Jennifer Abele started out as an entry-level budget analyst for the City of Milwaukee before working her way up to become the city's primary in-house lobbyist. Ron Book lives in Aventura, Florida, and represents a variety of local governments, including cities, counties, and special districts, as well as private clients. And Dana Fenton dreamed of becoming a city manager before realizing that he had a knack for intergovernmental lobbying. After working for Johnson County in Kansas and Prince William County in Virginia, he accepted a job working for the City of Charlotte, North Carolina, where he serves as the chief intergovernmental relations manager.

The book is organized as follows. In the second chapter, I draw from original lobbying disclosure data, interviews, city council meeting minutes, and other sources to paint a detailed descriptive picture of the current municipal lobbying landscape in the United States. How did city lobbying emerge in its current form? What are local officials hoping to achieve when they lobby, and how do they allocate their efforts? When do cities lobby as individuals as opposed to coalitions? This chapter introduces expansive new data to provide initial answers to these questions.

After laying this descriptive groundwork, in Chapter 3 I flesh out my theoretical argument about how intergovernmental lobbying can compensate for the representational gaps that sometimes emerge across different levels of government. I then test several observable implications of this theory using original panel data on annual city lobbying activity in all fifty states. The longitudinal nature of the data makes it possible to examine the lobbying decisions of the same cities over time, which allows me to draw more robust inferences about the causes of lobbying than would be possible with a cross-sectional sample.

Using a series of research designs that take advantage of the fact that cities start and stop lobbying at different times, I show that municipal officials hire lobbyists in response to a wide array of representational challenges. For example, cities are more likely to lobby when they are redistricted in a way that changes the composition of their state legislative delegation and when their district representatives diverge from local residents in terms of partisanship. However, I also find that city size and economic resources are major determinants of the decision to lobby. This chapter begins to highlight some of the normative tensions inherent to the market for intergovernmental representation. While lobbying appears to provide an important channel through which local officials can attempt to correct certain representational imbalances, smaller and less affluent communities are less likely to take advantage of this opportunity.

Having established some of the individual factors that lead cities to pay for lobbying services, in the fourth chapter I zoom out to examine the state-level features that are associated with differences in the intensity of local government lobbying. Several state characteristics correlate with municipal lobbying, such as local property tax limitations, but two of the most striking are the combination of term limits and the level of professionalization in the state legislature. Cities are also more likely to mobilize as state transfers comprise a greater share of municipal budgets. These findings suggest that lobbyists might be particularly useful at facilitating representation in complex legislative environments with high turnover among elected officials—especially when cities depend on the state for revenue.

In the second half of the book, I turn to the question of how city lobbying shapes state spending and policy outcomes. In Chapter 5, I use a variety of panel data methods to estimate the returns to lobbying for individual municipalities. I find that when cities start lobbying, they receive significantly more revenue from the state in the following year compared to other cities. But not all localities benefit equally. In particular, wealthy communities with higher median incomes tend to receive substantially more revenue after lobbying than less affluent municipalities. The chapter concludes by discussing some of the mechanisms that might be driving these results. While higher-income cities don't spend more money on lobbying, they do spread their efforts across a greater number of bills, and they appear to be particularly savvy at using their lobbyists to advocate for shovel-ready projects that make attractive funding targets for state officials.

In Chapter 6, I consider how city lobbying affects the overall policy environment from the perspective of the state. While the city-level results in Chapter 5 suggest that there are individual winners and losers from the lobbying process, this chapter shows how aggregate lobbying trends can systematically bias state transfers toward the interests of high-income cities, making them less progressive on average. At the same time, local officials don't lobby for funding alone. Through a series of short case studies, this chapter also examines how the lobbying efforts of cities are shaping current policy debates in state legislatures, including preemption battles over minimum wage laws. While difficult to quantify the effects of these activities, taking a more holistic view of city lobbying paints a more nuanced and positive picture about its policy consequences.

The final chapter concludes by considering the broader welfare implications of the intergovernmental lobbying system that has emerged in the United States. How does the ability to pay for lobbying services help or hurt the quality of intergovernmental representation from the perspective of citizens, local leaders, and state officials? The answer is complicated. On the one hand, municipal lobbying plays a vital role in facilitating the exchange of information between state and local governments. Lobbyists can help cities communicate their needs and achieve their goals in the state legislature, and state officials benefit from being provided with information about the preferences of their constituents. At the same time, affluent cities have become particularly adept at lobbying, and they appear to capture more state funding as a result.

I conclude that in order to assess the net policy effects of municipal lobbying and discuss possible avenues for reform, it's important to understand why paying for lobbyist representation has become so ubiquitous for cities in the first place. How did we end up with a system where political officials in different levels of government often choose to pay professional lobbyists to facilitate communication between them? As I demonstrate throughout this book, the answer is deeply rooted in both the nature of our federal system and the evolution of the lobbying industry. Cities shoulder enormous responsibilities in terms of providing public services, but they are also heavily dependent on the policy and funding decisions of their state governments. Given their political geography, cities experience strong incentives to lobby—and this has become synonymous with hiring professional lobbyists as the lobbying industry has exploded at the state level over the past few decades.

In a political environment characterized by intense urban-rural polarization and growing hostility between many cities and state governments, lobbyists play a crucial role facilitating intergovernmental advocacy. Local officials from municipalities both large and small claim that their ability to lobby is a critical tool to help them perform their jobs, and the motivation to lobby is built into the federal system. While some states have recently debated measures to restrict lobbying by local governments, I argue that these efforts would likely do more harm than good in the absence of substantial reform to the lobbying industry more generally. Otherwise, the influence of corporations and PACs will almost certainly continue to grow, while local officials would unfairly lose one of the key channels through which they are able to advocate for local interests at the state level.

Cities are some of the oldest lobbying organizations in the country, and their role in shaping the state policy environment only appears to be increasing in the twenty-first century. Professional lobbyists have become deeply intertwined with this process, and it is unlikely that this will change anytime soon. To understand who has access to power in our federal system, it's crucial that scholars start paying more attention to the lobbying decisions of local actors. The wealth of new data and empirical discoveries offered in this volume offer a starting point to scholars and practitioners who want to engage with these questions.

2

The State of Local Lobbying

Some of the most powerful attempts to influence decisions are directed by government officials against other government officials.
—Milbrath, *The Washington Lobbyists* (1963)

When nobody was representing local government, we started representing local governments. We felt they were entitled to the same type of representation that private-sector clients were receiving.
—Lobbyist Ron Book, Tallahassee, Florida

Upon its completion in 1825, the Erie Canal became the second longest man-made waterway in the world. Its construction allowed huge shipments of wheat and other agricultural commodities to be distributed along the East Coast and exported to Europe. The canal contributed to a series of fundamental social and economic changes in the United States that shaped nineteenth-century settlement patterns, launched New York's rise as the financial capital of the world, and provided the North with critical supply line advantages during the Civil War. And yet, it took nearly four decades for state and federal officials to openly endorse the project, with Thomas Jefferson initially dismissing it as "little short of madness."[1]

The catalyst that eventually led to construction of the iconic canal? Intensive lobbying of the New York State Legislature by the municipal officials and local boosters of Buffalo, Rochester, Syracuse, and New York City. After being rebuffed by the federal government for funding, the cities turned their attention to their elected officials in the statehouse. The newly appointed governor DeWitt Clinton was also sympathetic to the cause—he was the former mayor of New York City, after all—and in 1817 the legislature voted to allocate $7 million from the state budget toward the project. Civic leaders in other cities quickly followed suit, lobbying the state assemblies of Pennsylvania, Maryland, Virginia, North Carolina, and South Carolina to request funding for expensive canal projects. Over 3,000 miles of canals were built between 1824 and 1840, and most of them were financed by state governments (Goodrich 1960).

The story of the Erie Canal is just one example of how city interests can shape state policy. In fact, some of the earliest documented lobbying activities in the United States were organized by cities petitioning their state legislatures (Berman 2003). Because states historically have enjoyed high levels of fiscal and administrative authority over their local units, local officials have always had strong incentives to participate in state politics. In the mid to late 1800s, courts consistently resolved disputes between state and local governments by invoking Dillon's Rule, a legal doctrine holding that municipalities "owe their origin to, and derive their powers and rights wholly from, the legislature." While some states also experimented with home rule, which theoretically granted more autonomy to local governments, in practice this distinction made little difference. The historian Charles Beard observed in 1912, "Shrewd legislatures, if supported by judicial sanction, may pass a great deal of [legislation affecting cities] under the guise of general acts, in spite of home-rule charters."[2] To advance their local agendas, cities almost always required state support. As a result, city officials and their lobbyists were some of the most active supplicants in state legislatures in the nineteenth century.

In *The Unheralded Triumph: City Government in America, 1870–1900*, John Teaford describes how municipal lobbyists would board trains to their state capitols and engulf the senate and house with requests for new local laws authorizing the paving of streets, the construction of municipal utilities, and changes to mayoral powers. State legislatures of this era were parochial and unprofessionalized and relied heavily on local government officials for information about constituency demands. By the late nineteenth century, cities were actively involved in shaping the state legislative environment. As Judd and Swanstrom (2015) explain, "Even if they had wanted to, state legislatures could not have been completely insulated from the political battles occurring in cities. Local governments provided key public services, and representatives to state legislatures answered to local constituents; as a consequence, local and state affairs were closely entwined" (93). Burns and Gamm (1997) add, "The ordinary work of state politics was local affairs, and an ordinary branch of local government was the state legislature" (90).

Despite its historical prevalence, we know relatively little about how lobbying by local governments shapes politics and policy in the modern era. Formative research in this area dates to the 1960s and 1970s, when scholars like Farkas (1971) and Haider (1974) studied how local government associations like the US Conference of Mayors and National Association of Counties sought to influence federal legislation and urban policy starting around the time of the New Deal. Since these initial efforts, a small body of largely qualitative research has continued to examine the causes and consequences of lobbying activities by government associations, usually at the federal level.[3] But in general, while the interest group literature often acknowledges that governments lobby each other (e.g., Milbrath 1963; Cigler 1995; Baumgartner and Leech 1998), most of this work instead focuses on the mobilization, tactics, and success of corporate lobbyists (e.g., Drutman 2015) or membership-based groups like the NRA and teachers unions (e.g., Hojnacki et al. 2012). In fact, many foundational studies explicitly excluded local governments (e.g., Schlozman and Tierney 1983), leading Grossmann (2013) to conclude that our understanding of intergovernmental lobbying remains "the largest hole in the mobilization literature" (61).

In contrast to the relative lack of attention given to local governments as lobbyists, research on lobbying more generally has advanced significantly in recent years. Data on lobbying activity have become more widely available as a result of stricter, more transparent regulations—especially at the federal level—and improved econometric techniques have allowed researchers to uncover important empirical regularities about the lobbying process. We now have more evidence than ever before about which organizations lobby, how lobbying works, and the consequences of this behavior on public policy.[4]

These lobbying disclosure records also offer a unique opportunity to study how local governments exercise power and seek to influence other levels of government. At the federal level, these reports have been collected since the passage of the 1995 Lobbying Disclosure Act and are readily available via the Senate Lobbying Disclosure Act Database. This law defines lobbying as any oral or written communication directed to a government official and providing input on legislation, rules and regulations, federal programs and policies, or political appointments.[5] Any person or organization that engages in this behavior is required to register and report on their efforts to influence at quarterly intervals. The vast majority of research on lobbying focuses on federal lobbying and uses these quarterly reports.

Each state also has its own disclosure law requiring lobbyists to report their communication with state officeholders—and each state law is at least as restrictive as the Federal Lobbying Disclosure Act (Lowery and Brasher 2004). But while every state regulates lobbying, this information is more difficult to access because each state has its own reporting standards.[6] Some make their lobbying information publicly available online; others are less transparent and only provide data upon request—and sometimes for a fee.

This lack of systematic state-level data has been a barrier for researchers interested in studying local governments as lobbyists. While federal lobbying is dominated by business interests and corporations (Drutman 2015), local government lobbying is more common at the state level. In Texas, over half of the 1,741 registered lobbyists in the 2015 legislative session were working in some capacity for local governments, including counties, school districts, water boards, and cities.[7] And in California, local governments have spent more on lobbying than any other interest group industry since at least 1999, the first year for which data are available via the Secretary of State website (Figure 2.1).

2.1 Using Disclosure Data to Document Local Influence

Many of the analyses in this book are the product of a multi-year data collection project that involved gathering, cleaning, and compiling lobbying disclosure data from all fifty states. Some states, like California, Washington, Idaho, and New York, post the names of all clients, lobbyists, and lobbying activity for each legislative session online in easy-to-access spreadsheets. Other states provide this information in PDF format, making it more difficult to extract and clean the relevant data. And some states, like New Hampshire, simply upload thousands of individual filings—some handwritten—which required manually entering the names of lobbying clients.

There are a few things to note about using disclosure filings to measure lobbying. First, there are some minor differences in the way that lobbying is defined across states. Most state laws require disclosure of attempts to influence either the legislature or the executive branch, but a few (including Oregon) cover only legislative advocacy. New York and Arizona go a step further and collect information on efforts to influence quasi-judicial activity, like obtaining permits and licenses. In some states, the lobbyist is solely responsible for filing the disclosure reports, while in others, the client (or

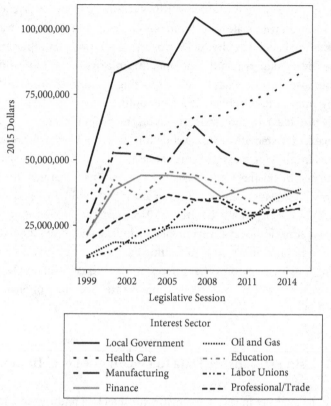

Figure 2.1 Lobbying Expenditures in California. For over fifteen years, local governments have spent more money lobbying in California than any other interest group sector.

Source: http://cal-access.sos.ca.gov/.

"lobbyist employer") is also required to register and file. In the chapter appendix, I describe the sources and the structure of the data and discuss the steps that I take to account for differences in state lobbying laws in the analyses that appear throughout the book.

Importantly, cities in every state are required to disclose the lobbying activities of both in-house employees as well as external firms. For example, if a large city hires a full-time staff member to lobby on its behalf, it needs to report that information. In general, these "in-house" advocates are also professional lobbyists, and they operate in a similar capacity as the professional attorneys that fill the in-house counsel positions of corporations. Dana Fenton, the intergovernmental affairs director of Charlotte, North Carolina, told me that he sometimes hires contract lobbyists to bolster his advocacy efforts and that he views the contract lobbyists as being an extension of his staff. Of the one hundred largest cities, seventy-two employ in-house lobbyists, but this rate falls dramatically among smaller cities. As a former county commissioner in Michigan explained, "We're just not large enough, and we don't have enough issues on the table on a day-to-day basis to pay for our own intergovernmental affairs staff."[8] A 2016 report issued by the Office of the Auditor in Minnesota revealed that 89 percent of local governments in the state rely solely on contract lobbyists, while 8 percent used both in-house and contract lobbyists, and 4 percent used in-house counsel alone.

Of course, it's always possible that lobbyists and their clients might try to skirt the system and fail to disclose their attempts to influence. But due to the often visible nature of their work, lobbyists are generally transparent about the clients they represent. Most legislative advocates view disclosure as both an ethical and legal duty, and their professional reputation depends on maintaining the trust of their clients and the elected officials they work with. As California lobbyist Anthony Gonsalves told me, "We've never misled a member of the legislature. It only takes an advocate one time to mislead a member of the legislature, and they'll talk about it in caucus. Every single member of the legislature will know, 'that advocate misled me.'"[9]

However, things become a bit dicier when it comes to more granular details on lobbying activity. While all states collect basic information about which lobbyists are representing which clients, major differences emerge when it comes to tracking spending and the specific bills and agencies that are being lobbied. In other words, we can typically determine with a high degree of confidence which organizations are lobbying in a given time period by relying on lobbying disclosure records, but it's much more difficult to consistently identify their lobbying goals or how much money they spent. To account for this, many of the analyses throughout the book rely on binary measures of lobbying that simply indicate if a local government lobbied the state government or not during a given period. I supplement this approach by occasionally zooming in on particular subsets of states with reliable expenditure data.

The combined disclosure reports yielded a dataset of nearly half a million observations of state lobbying activity between 2006 and 2015, although some states have data going back as far as 2000. Armed with information about all of the organizations that were lobbying in a given state in each year, I identified which cities employed lobbyists by matching the client names in the disclosure data with the universe of municipalities enumerated by the Census of Governments. The Census of Governments is conducted every five years by the Census Bureau with the goal of identifying every operational subnational government in the United States. It also collects detailed information on local finances as well as public employment statistics.[10]

Throughout the book, I'll generally treat "cities" as though they are unitary actors. Of course, cities actually consist of a variety of different decision makers—including mayors, city council members, city managers, and staff members—who may or may not have a unified vision of how they want to run their governments. Jennifer Abele, the in-house lobbyist for Milwaukee, Wisconsin, emphasized that one of her jobs was to gather input and resolve differences across the intergovernmental priorities of the department heads. But, fundamentally, the job of both contract lobbyists and intergovernmental affairs liaisons is to craft a consolidated legislative agenda to guide their advocacy efforts. The mayor or the city manager is typically the person who signs off on this agenda, often after obtaining city council approval. For the purposes of simplicity, I'll often refer to "the city" as the unit of observation, which is a common simplifying approach in the urban political economy literature.

After determining which city governments filed state disclosure reports, I merged this information with federal lobbying records as well as financial, demographic, and political data from dozens of other sources. These include the American Community Survey, municipal elections data (De Benedictis-Kessner and Warshaw 2016), Missouri Census Center geography data, state legislator ideology estimates (Shor and McCarty 2015), city ideology estimates (Tausanovitch and Warshaw 2014), and information from the National Center for Money in State Politics, to name a few. The primary dataset that resulted from this process contains information about municipal lobbying activity and city characteristics over time for each of the roughly 4,500 cities in the United States that have a population above 5,000 residents.[11] The appendix to this chapter contains additional details for each state, including the years of available data, the number of cities and the proportion that disclose lobbying activity, and whether lobbying expenditure information exists.

The state-level lobbying disclosure data reveal that cities are not the only local governments that hire lobbyists. Between 2006 and 2015, there were 461 school districts, 570 counties, 1,510 cities, and 2,033 special districts that lobbied their statehouses at some point (Figure 2.2). Other than special

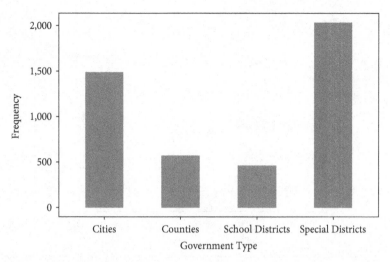

Figure 2.2 Total Local Government Lobbying by Type, 2006–2015. Cities are the most common type of state government lobbyist after special districts. More cities lobby than counties or school districts.

districts, which are extremely heterogeneous and often difficult to map geographically, municipalities are the most common government lobbyists at the state level. While some of the findings in this book likely generalize to other types of local governments, the lobbying behavior of cities is important in its own right—particularly in a political moment where cities are facing extraordinary challenges to their autonomy from state legislatures.

2.2 Targeting the State vs. Federal Government

Existing studies of intergovernmental lobbying have focused primarily on lobbying in Washington, DC.[12] But Figure 2.3 indicates that state lobbying was nearly twice as common for cities as federal lobbying between 2006 and 2015. It's not surprising that local officials focus most of their advocacy efforts at the state level. Cities rely heavily on their state governments for funding, with state transfers comprising 32 percent of the average city's budget in 2015. In contrast, only 4 percent of municipal revenue comes directly from the federal government.[13] And, bills in state legislatures are also disproportionately likely to affect city government, which I discuss in more detail later in this chapter.

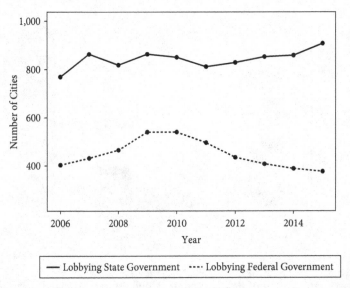

Figure 2.3 Cities Lobbying the State and Federal Government. Between 2006 and 2015, cities lobbied their state government at roughly twice the rate that they lobbied the federal government.

One thing to note about Figure 2.3 is that there appears to be a slight up-tick in the number of cities lobbying the federal government in the years 2009 and 2010, coinciding with the passage of the American Recovery and Reinvestment Act. This fiscal stimulus package was designed to jump-start the economy following the Great Recession and included billions of dollars in assistance for local governments. In response, an increasing number of local governments turned to professional lobbyists in a bid to increase their share of the aid. As the director for intergovernmental affairs in Miami-Dade explained, "With the type of money coming out of Washington with the stimulus, how can you afford not to keep your lobbying corps at full strength?"[14]

This book focuses primarily on the period between 2006 and 2015, when the bulk of quantitative data are available at the state level. As a result, the following chapters are designed to explore the causes and consequences of city lobbying in the important decade leading up to the 2016 election. But histor-ical sources suggest cities were lobbying for decades before comprehensive disclosure data became available, with their reliance on professional lobbyists burgeoning as the state-level lobbying industry expanded in the 1980s.

At the federal level, individual cities began formally lobbying around the time of the New Deal, when cash-strapped local governments sought to compete for newly available revenue for public works projects (Haider 1974; Flanagan 1999). The Federal Emergency Relief Administration provided $500 million—over $9.25 billion in 2016 dollars—to states and cities, and President Roosevelt actively encouraged local governments to vie for the cash by promoting the merits of local projects (Cammisa 1995). This trend continued throughout the era of Johnson's Great Society program as federal grants were channeled to cities to address issues like slum clearance, community development, and urban renewal. By the end of 1974, local authorities had received federal support for more than 2,100 city renewal projects. When Congress began formally documenting federal lobbying efforts in the mid-1990s, local governments had a long track record of competing for federal funding and seeking to influence policy.[15]

At the state level, historical records indicate that local government lobbying dates back at least to the mid-nineteenth century, when city boosters began actively trying to influence the location of railroads and canals. Many of these early advocacy efforts involved local officials working directly with their elected delegations (Gamm and Kousser 2013) or via urban party coalitions (Weir, Wolman, and Swanstrom 2005). California state legislators undertook one of the first systematic efforts to document this behavior in the 1950s. In 1951, the State Assembly created an Interim Committee on Municipal and County Government after it came to the attention of lawmakers that certain county governments were spending money on "legislative advocacy." The committee found that fifty-four out of fifty-eight counties engaged in either direct or indirect lobbying of the state legislature and concluded that "there may be question as to the propriety of the use of county taxpayers money in attempts to influence legislation."[16]

Statehouse lobbying in the modern era took off in the 1980s as Ronald Reagan gradually transferred autonomy for social programs back to the states. From the 1960s to 1980s, the institutional capabilities of state legislatures increased dramatically as they experimented with reforms designed to professionalize the policymaking process. While the so-called devolution revolution gave states more discretion over public spending, it also curtailed the amount of federal money available. Cities now had to look to their states to secure funding, and this tendency only became more pronounced after Republicans gained control of Congress in 1994 for the first time in decades (Danielson and Lewis 1996; Freeman and Nownes 1999; Conlan 2006).

These new incentives for local governments to participate in state politics coincided with the dramatic expansion of the lobbying industry at the state level. In his classic book *The Third House: Lobbyists and Lobbying in the States*, Rosenthal (1993) attributed this growth to the increasing size and complexity of state government, as well as to an influx of professional lobbyists trickling down from DC. Prior to the 1970s, very few interest groups employed professional lobbyists. Most corporate lobbying was done through trade associations, and the goal was not so much to influence policy as to simply report back to headquarters (Milbrath 1963; Bauer, Pool, and Dexter 1963).[17] According to Marvin Leavitt, a former lobbyist for Las Vegas, "Back in the '70s and early '80s, we had very few governments who had lobbyists represent them full time in Carson City. They were normally the employees of the government who were sent up there to represent them at the Legislature."[18]

While few states kept formal records of professional lobbying activities before the 1990s, Minnesota is an exception. In a report prepared for the Minnesota state legislature in 1989, analysts commented that lobbying by local governments had increased dramatically since 1977, with the number of local governments hiring lobbyists tripling between 1977 and 1983 and then further doubling from 1983 to 1989. The report notes that the increasing complexity of the property tax system and state funding formulas likely contributed to this phenomenon, as they resulted in more local dependence on the state.[19]

Similarly, local government lobbying in California proliferated after the adoption of local property tax limitations in the late 1970s.[20] As Anthony Gonslaves recalls, "When I first started lobbying back in 1977, there were lobbyists for Oakland, Los Angeles, San Francisco, San Jose, and San Diego. There was no body representing the small- and medium-sized cities except for the League of Cities."[21] Municipalities in other states soon followed suit. Ron Book began taking on local government clients in Florida in the 1990s, and the first mayor to hire a lobbyist in Utah did so in 1994.[22] By the early 2000s, professional advocates were regularly representing cities in states across the country.

Cities lobby both their states and the federal government—and sometimes both at once. Table 2.1 breaks down instances of city lobbying by level of government between 2006 and 2015. The majority of the time (53%), cities lobbied only their state government in a given year without lobbying the federal government. Lobbying both levels of government was also common, with cities doing this 31 percent of the time. Only 16 percent of city-year

Table 2.1 Cities Lobbying State vs. Federal Government. Between 2006 and 2015, the majority of city lobbying was aimed at the state government alone (53%), while 31% targeted both levels. Only 16% of city-year lobbying observations targeted the federal government alone.

	City-Year Lobbying Observations	
	N	%
State Only	4,724	53
State and Federal	2,809	31
Federal Only	1,435	16

lobbying observations were directed at the federal government alone. While the following chapters focus on state-level lobbying, explaining why cities choose to lobby the state versus the federal government deserves further investigation in future research.

2.3 Who Advocates for Cities?

Who are the professional advocates that have come to play such an instrumental role in representing the interests of cities in state politics? Intergovernmental lobbyists often boast prior experience working as elected officials or staff members at either the state or local level. Joe Gonsalves (Anthony's father) launched his career as an advocate for California cities after first serving as a council member for the newly incorporated City of Dairy Valley, followed by twelve years in the State Assembly. After he lost his state re-election bid in 1974, Gonsalves recalled talking to a friend and realizing that he might make a good lobbyist. "I've been in [Sacramento] for 12 years. I know the system. I know the people. They're friends of mine. I know most of the staff, so wouldn't that be natural for me to represent people at the Capitol who have problems that they don't know how to handle themselves?"[23]

Similarly, Neal "Buddy" Jones was elected as county prosecutor in Hill County, Texas, before moving to the Texas House of Representatives and eventually founding the lobbying firm HillCo, whose clients include cities like Fort Worth and Houston. In Michigan, Kirk Profit worked in the Washtenaw County Sheriff Department before serving in the House of Representatives for ten years. He then joined the advocacy firm GCSI, which represents a number of municipalities in Washtenaw County, including Ann Arbor. Finally, Jennifer Abele became the in-house lobbyist for Milwaukee after working as a budget analyst for the city. In that role, she realized that "Most of our constraints as a local government were a result of either policies at the state level or restrictions or reductions on state aid. I became increasingly frustrated with my internally facing role working on municipal finance because I didn't really feel like we had the tools to resolve the structural deficits that we were seeing every year."[24]

Intergovernmental lobbying firms typically specialize in representing local governments, although larger firms might have a substantial number of private-sector clients as well. To avoid conflicts of interest between their cities, the lobbyists I spoke to said that they often strive to represent particular types of local governments that are similar in terms of size or geography. As Anthony Gonsalves explained, "We try to keep our client cities similar fiscally." His son, Jason, added, "It's not by accident that we haven't had many conflicts. When asked to represent the larger cities, when asked to represent counties—and in some cases even special districts—we've declined doing so because they don't fit with the fiscal structure and makeup of our client cities. If we get a request to represent the city neighboring an existing client, we'd call the City Manager and make sure there's no underlying conflicts that we should be aware of."[25]

2.4   Where Cities Lobby

I assume (and later provide qualitative evidence) that the goal of municipal lobbying is to influence state policy in a way that benefits local interests. But all local governments should want this type of favorable treatment. Why is it that some cities hire lobbyists to help them achieve these objectives while others don't? This is the question addressed in Chapter 3. But one feature that distinguishes cities that are likely to lobby is so central that it's worth mentioning here. In general, cities that employ lobbyists tend to be major metropolitan cores. Table 2.2 highlights the relationship between population

Table 2.2 City Lobbying by Population. As city
population increases, lobbying becomes more common.
Regardless of size, cities are more likely to lobby their state
than the federal government.

		% Lobbying	
Population	N	State	Federal
5,000–20,000	2,899	6	2
20,001–50,000	994	20	9
50,001–100,000	431	43	27
100,001–500,000	242	71	52
Over 500,000	33	78	77

and the likelihood of lobbying. Size is clearly an important factor in the decision to lobby. While only 6 percent of municipalities with between 5,000
and 20,000 residents lobby their state governments, that proportion grows
steadily as city population increases, with the large majority of cities with
over 100,000 residents lobbying. Note that across cities of all sizes, lobbying
the state government is more common than lobbying Washington, DC—
although this gap decreases among the largest municipalities.

This finding mirrors an empirical regularity in the corporate lobbying literature, which finds that firm size is one of the most consistent predictors
of corporate political activity (Grier, Munger, and Roberts 1994; Hillman,
Keim, and Schuler 2004; Drope and Hansen 2006). Theoretical explanations
for this phenomenon typically emphasize that larger companies are disproportionately impacted by the political and economic environment and thus
face greater incentives to shape that environment through lobbying and PAC
contributions (Mitchell, Hansen, and Jepsen 1997). At the same time, these
companies also have more resources at their disposal to engage in political
activities. A similar logic likely applies to cities. Larger cities face greater
demand for services and are especially sensitive to changes in state policies
(Zimmerman 2012). In the next chapter, I provide more formal evidence of
the relationship between municipal size and the decision to lobby, as well as
other city characteristics that contribute to this behavior.

City lobbying is common across the United States and is not limited to a
single state or region. Figure 2.4 maps every city with a population of 20,000

Figure 2.4 Geographic Distribution of Lobbying Cities, Population 20,000+. City lobbying is widespread across the United States and is not limited to a single state or region.

or more and shows which cities disclosed lobbying activity at least once between 2006 and 2015. Cities hire lobbyists in every state except Hawaii, with particularly high rates of municipal mobilization in Washington, California, Texas, and Florida. States also experience significant variation in the proportion of cities that lobby. Table A2.2 in the chapter appendix contains additional details about the number of cities per state and the proportion that lobby. Municipal lobbying appears to be more common in the West and relatively infrequent in the Mid-Atlantic states. But the majority of states experience lobbying by at least 25 percent of their cities.

Figure 2.4 suggests some intriguing trends about the state-level conditions that lead to city lobbying. The more fragmented states east of the Mississippi River tend to have lots of small, densely situated municipalities and relatively few cities that lobby. On the other hand, the West has fewer total cities that are more spread out geographically—but a higher proportion of those cities lobby. States also vary in terms of how professionalized their legislatures are, how dependent cities are for state funding, whether they have term limits, and a host of other factors. Chapter 4 delves more systematically into explaining this variation across states.

2.5 What Cities Want

After conducting interviews with the leaders of several big cities in Illinois, Michigan, Ohio, and New York about their relationship with the state government, Weir, Wolman, and Swanstrom (2005) drew two conclusions: "(1) Cities want legal autonomy from state interferences, and (2) cities want more money from the state either directly in the form of state grants or indirectly in the form of state-funded capital projects that will enhance local tax collections" (747). Local governments provide a unique window into the goals of organizations that lobby. This is because various open-meeting statutes across all fifty states require local governments to perform their business in a manner accessible to the public (Fernandes 2009). As a result, cities often leave detailed paper trails documenting their lobbying priorities. These records can be found in city council meeting minutes, city archives, and public reports.

Cities are generally transparent about their lobbying objectives. As Weir, Wolman, and Swanstrom (2005) observe, they want more money, greater autonomy, fewer mandates, and increased institutional power. Many cities publicly post their lobbying contracts on their city council websites, along with detailed descriptions of the proposed services. By way of example, Figure A2.1 in the chapter appendix is an excerpt from a report filed by the city manager of Palo Alto, California. The report explicitly states that the city intends to hire a lobbyist to "protect local revenue sources," "protect and increase funding for specific programs and services," and "oppose legislation, policies and budgets that reduce the authority and/or ability of local government to determine how best to effectively operate local programs," among other goals.

In general, the lobbying aims of cities can be divided into three primary categories. The first is legislative lobbying, which consists of supporting and opposing specific bills, seeking to influence the state budgeting and appropriations process, and attempting to procure earmarks. Second, cities lobby the executive branch and state agencies in order to secure grants and shape regulations. Finally, city officials use lobbyists as monitors, where the goal is not to exert influence but simply to get information about potential state actions so that cities can proactively prepare. In the following sections, I discuss each of these strategies in turn.[26]

2.5.1 Lobbying the Legislature

First and foremost, local governments lobby their state legislatures to sup-port and oppose laws with local consequences. In 2014, the Texas Municipal League estimated that almost 1,500 bills or resolutions of the 7,000 that were introduced (25%) would have "substantially" impacted Texas cities.[27] In California, over a third of bills introduced during the 1990s had implications for local government operations (Freeman and Nownes 1999). Today, leg-islation in forty-two states restricts the ability of local governments to raise revenue via tax and expenditure limitations, and twenty-four states have enacted preemption laws that constrain cities from passing minimum wage ordinances.[28] Given the local impacts of so many of these policies, cities have strong incentives to try to shape state legislation. Lobbyists are aware of this, and many lobbying firms include a "Legislative Accomplishments" section on their websites highlighting recent bills that they claim to have successfully blocked or helped to become law.

To better understand what types of bills municipal officials are lobbying on behalf of, I examined the universe of 1,361 lobbying disclosure reports filed by cities in California during the 2015–2016 legislative session. The two pieces of legislation that cities were by far the most likely to lobby were the State Budget Act of 2015 and State Budget Act of 2016. Ron Book said the same thing was true in Florida: "Once you understand how the budget works, you learn that there are many opportunities for government-to-government advocacy. But if no one's here advocating, if you're a local government and you don't use the 'A' word and ask, you don't get anything."[29] Municipalities in California also enumerated 956 individual bills that they lobbied for during this session. Most of these bills originated in either the Appropriations Committee (30%), the Budget and Fiscal Review Committee (10%), or the Local Government Committee (10%). These bills tended to focus on policy areas of particular interest to local governments, including transportation, housing, infrastructure, and water policy.

It's important to note that much intergovernmental lobbying is defen-sive. One lobbyist for the Texas Municipal League estimated that in a typ-ical session, the League tries to get about twenty-five bills passed and about a thousand killed. "If we didn't pass a single thing and nothing bad passed, we would have a good session."[30] The lobbyists and local officials that I spoke to echoed this sentiment over and over again. According to Dana Fenton, the intergovernmental affairs director of Charlotte, North Carolina, "You might achieve some of your legislative agenda, but the most important thing is blocking harmful measures and not losing local authority."[31]

In addition to lobbying for or against legislation that would impact them locally, cities also frequently lobby for legislative earmarks. The 2015 California Budget contained dozens of such earmarks, which amounted to millions of dollars in funding to renovate bridges, expand parks, and open new health clinics.[32] The City of Corcoran, introduced in Chapter 1, used the earmarked funds it secured via lobbying to build a new police station. In other states, some cities have come to rely on earmarks as a primary source of revenue. Clearwater, Florida, managed to secure thirty-seven earmarks between 2001 and 2006, including $4 million to renovate its beach boardwalk and $1.5 million for a new homeless shelter. The city clerk attributed the city's success entirely to its lobbying firm, Alcade & Fay. "If we didn't have [them], we wouldn't be getting the funding we're getting."[33]

2.5.2 Executive Branch Lobbying

Local governments also lobby their state executive branches. Bureaucratic agencies are often responsible for administering grants, and one of the services that lobbyists advertise is their ability to help local officials craft their applications to secure these funds. Alcalde & Fay, the Florida firm representing Clearwater, sends its clients weekly emails detailing available grants for which the city is eligible.[34] And Townsend Public Affairs of California touts millions of dollars in grant funding for their government clients in the areas of transportation, water infrastructure, and housing development. According to the Townsend website, "with hundreds of programs and applications it is easy to get overwhelmed . . . [our firm] employs a targeted funding strategy that identifies city priorities, matches them with higher probability grants and authorizations, staffs the city through the application process, and employs legislative and departmental relationships to give cities a competitive advantage."[35]

In addition to lobbying for grants, cities often lobby agencies to shape state regulations. In California, one of the recent regulatory battles that cities have engaged with involves the sale and distribution of cannabis, which was legalized for recreational use in 2016. Initially, municipal governments enjoyed broad authority to license and regulate how companies could grow, test, and sell cannabis within their jurisdictional boundaries. But the Bureau of

Cannabis Control has since periodically threatened to centralize regulation and weaken this type of local control. Subsequently, many cities have started mentioning cannabis regulation as a goal of their lobbying efforts, including Sacramento, Desert Hot Spring, Emeryville, and Oakland.[36]

2.5.3 Lobbying as Monitoring

Lobbying generally evokes the notion of influence. But according to city officeholders, one of the major reasons they hire lobbyists is simply to gather information about the actions of other levels of government. Rather than advocating for new policy, funding, and regulatory decisions, local lobbyists are often tasked with alerting their clients to potential changes in the policy environment so that cities can prepare themselves. "One of the benefits for us was (the lobbyist) kept a really close tab on any new bills that were being proposed that could affect [us], either positively or negatively," explained Brian Oaks, a local official in Springfield, Illinois.[37]

Some cities specifically stipulate a monitoring role in their lobbying contracts. El Paso, Texas, requested that its lobbying firm, Focused Advocacy, "submit monthly written reports to the Mayor, City Council, and City manager . . . so as to allow the City Council to make informed decisions relative to legislative matters."[38] These reports typically provide a summary of upcoming issues on the docket—from immigration policy to property tax caps to smoking bans—and often analyze the local implications of the proposed policy changes. The City of Rockville, Maryland, stipulates even more frequent reports when the legislature is in session and emphasizes that one of the major roles of its lobbying firm is to simply be available on a "real-time basis" to keep the city aware of legislative developments.[39]

Local officeholders frequently mention the importance of having "eyes and ears on the ground" and argue that professional lobbyists provide them with essential information about developments in the statehouse.[40] Florida lobbyist Ron Book put it bluntly: "You cannot expect local government officials who are often working part-time or aren't compensated for their service to come and spend 60 consecutive days away from their families and their jobs when the legislature is in session."[41] A popular saying in politics quips that if you aren't at the table, you're on the menu. Many cities view their lobbyists as a way to ensure that they can mobilize quickly in the rapidly changing world of state politics.

2.6 Allocating Lobbying Effort: Evidence from Florida

Most states require organizations to register and disclose their lobbying activities regardless of whether they are lobbying the legislative or executive
branch. But the majority of states do not differentiate between these two
types of lobbying in their public disclosure data. One exception is Florida,
which specifically documents whether lobbying efforts are aimed at legislative or executive officials. Figure 2.5 shows the number of cities lobbying
either the state legislature or the executive branch in the period from 2007
to 2015.

According to the data, legislative advocacy is more common, but cities
actively lobby both branches. In New York, which also requires lobbying
entities to detail both their legislative and executive branch activity, every
city listed the state legislature, and most mentioned the governor's office and
various state agencies as well.[42] In a survey of Kansas lobbyists, 70 percent
of respondents claimed they spent four-fifths or more of their time lobbying
legislators as opposed to the executive branch (Nownes and Freeman 1998).

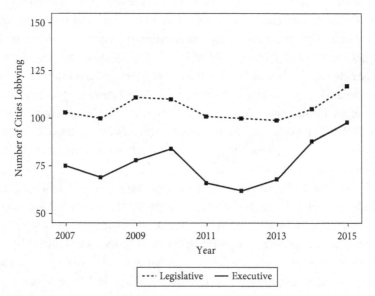

Figure 2.5 Legislative vs. Executive Branch Lobbying in Florida. Cities lobby
both the legislative and executive branches of state government. In Florida,
cities reported lobbying the legislature roughly 30 percent more often than the
executive branch.

Monitoring is even harder to quantify, as this type of activity does not need to be reported in any state unless it accompanies attempts to influence. But most city officials I spoke to said that receiving information from lobbyists was an added benefit of hiring them rather than the primary purpose. In general, the quantitative analyses in this volume are unable to distinguish between these different types of lobbying. All of these tactics appear to be common and closely linked, and qualitative evidence suggests that cities often pursue multiple strategies as they seek to adapt to the state political environment.

2.7 Banding Together or Going It Alone? The Role of Municipal Leagues

This book primarily examines the lobbying behavior of individual city governments. But it is important to note that virtually all cities lobby— at least indirectly—by virtue of participating in their state municipal leagues. Around 95 percent of municipalities pay dues to their state municipal coalitions (De Soto 1995), from the League of California Cities to the Connecticut Conference of Municipalities. In fact, the only state without an association of cities is Hawaii, and the remaining forty-nine state municipal leagues are uniformly active as lobbyists in their respective state governments. Many cities also join smaller coalitions that represent the interests of local governments with similar geographic, financial, or demographic profiles. In Minnesota, for example, cities can choose between the League of Minnesota Cities, the Association of Metropolitan Municipalities, the Coalition of Greater Minnesota Cities, the Municipal Legislative Commission, and the League of Small Cities (Rosenthal 1993).

How do the lobbying goals of city leagues vary from the lobbying goals of individual municipalities? In some respects, the objectives are similar. State municipal league platforms all mention ensuring adequate funding for cities and opposing legislation that would reduce local authority. The Illinois League of Cities concisely summarizes these core principles as the following: 1. Maintain Local Control; 2. Preserve Home Rule Powers; 3. Oppose Unfunded Mandates; 4. Preserve the Rights of Municipalities to Decide Employee Wages and Benefits; and 5. Protect State-Shared Revenues. Some associations in other states also mention more specific policy goals, like addressing homelessness and expanding human services (Association of

Washington Cities) or reforming health insurance for municipal employees (Massachusetts Municipal Association).

The key difference between the lobbying activities of municipal leagues and those of individual cities is that leagues lobby for policies that would strengthen municipalities generally, while individual cities lobby for local benefits that would disproportionately impact them. As Illinois Municipal League member Tom Gray explains, "They [the Municipal League] lobby for major, across-the-board legislation that affects everybody equally. They can't lobby for you individually."[43] This is particularly true when members have diverging priorities. According to a spokesperson for the Rhode Island League of Cities and Towns, "Many issues pit the central city against suburban and rural towns [and this] puts the League in a tough position."[44]

Florida lobbyist Ron Book explained that one of his roles is to help cities with local issues when the Florida League of Cities can't take sides. "I tell my cities: you pay dues to the Florida League of Cities for a reason. They've got a team of in-house people, and they all hire outside people, and they can effectively handle global issues like a change to funding formulas. But you can't necessarily rely on the League of Cities to tout your particular, local project. There are too many cities for that."[45] Jason Gonsalves added that in California, "We don't try to duplicate what The League does. We work well with The League, but we take on the issues that you can't take to The League or that you can't take to one of your associations. It's individual, city-by-city issues that we address on an ongoing basis."[46]

To further investigate how the goals of individual cities and municipal leagues overlap or diverge, I gathered data from the State of Montana, which collects particularly detailed records of each bill that organizations lobby on behalf of. In 2015, the Montana League of Cities and Towns reported lobbying on sixty-five bills, while the largest city—Billings—lobbied for thirty-seven. Legislation supported by the League that Billings took no position on included broad-ranging policies like HJ28, which proposed a study on the effects of municipal collective bargaining. At the same time, Billings overlapped with the League on roughly half of the bills that it lobbied, typically on issues that had the potential to significantly affect Billings while also broadly impacting municipal government operations across the state. These measures involved changes to business tax laws, medical coverage rates for firefighters, and the regulation of municipal utilities. Finally, Billings also lobbied for several bills that the League did not take a position on. These proposals included particularistic projects like HB512, which was proposed legislation to provide funds to establish a state-of-the-art crime lab in Billings' county.

In his research on how cities attempt to influence state politics, De Soto (1995) uncovered a variety of additional examples of projects that cities found they could not pursue via their state leagues. Austin, Texas, wanted to move its city council elections to coincide with the state primary runoff. Lynn, Massachusetts, hoped to change the boundaries of its local port authority; Providence, Rhode Island, sought legal approval to establish a shopping mall; and Minneapolis, Minnesota, wanted funding to acquire a new arena for the city's NBA team. The following chapters focus on explaining the lobbying choices of individual cities—which often revolve around the pursuit of local projects like these.

2.8   Discussion

Across the United States, cities and other local governments actively seek to influence the policy and funding decisions of their states. And yet we know relatively little about the mechanics of intergovernmental lobbying. This chapter introduced expansive new data on city lobbying using state-level disclosure filings, allowing me to document a variety of novel facts about where and how cities lobby. Municipal officials hire lobbyists in every state, although states vary in the proportion of their cities that lobby. While cities lobby both their states and the federal government, state-level lobbying is significantly more common.

Intergovernmental lobbying in its contemporary form began to emerge during the New Deal era as subnational governments competed for an influx of federal funding. But since the 1980s, cities have become more reliant on their states for revenue, and states have significantly increased their fiscal and administrative authority over their local units. Cities also receive more than twenty times as much revenue from the state as from the federal government. As a result, it should not be surprising that the majority of municipal lobbying targets state government rather than Washington, DC. While historically cities tended to lobby informally by contacting their elected officials directly, the vast majority of lobbying today happens through contract lobbyists—or, for the largest cities, through lobbyists employed in-house.

There are three primary goals of municipal lobbying. Legislative lobbying is aimed at influencing the content of bills, the state budget, and the distribution of earmarks. Municipal lobbyists also target the executive branch to seek grants and shape the regulatory process. Finally, city officials rely on lobbyists to simply provide them with information about potential state actions so that they can prepare for changes to local policy and funding. Cities use each of these tactics frequently, and they appear to be largely intertwined.

Municipalities lobby both individually and as part of coalitions through their state municipal leagues. In fact, over 95 percent of cities pay dues to their state associations, which means that collective, indirect lobbying by municipalities is common. While large metropolitan centers are the most likely to lobby as individuals, cities of all sizes will occasionally choose to lobby as they attempt to increase their funding, autonomy, and institutional power. But all cities should want these things. Why do some local officials take the costly step of hiring a lobbyist while others don't? I turn to this question in the next chapter.

3

How City Lobbyists Bridge
Representational Gaps

People see their mayor and their elected state officials, and they don't
understand there's this whole other layer working behind the scenes.
We're the liaisons that help to make these relationships work.
—Intergovernmental Affairs Advocate Jennifer Abele,
Milwaukee, Wisconsin

It's important that the city has a lobbying presence in Harrisburg,
and it's doubly important that Philly, which is a Democratic city, has
access to GOP leadership who basically run the show.
—Lobbyist Larry Ceisler,
Philadelphia, Pennsylvania

Over the past decade, Charlotte, North Carolina, has emerged as a progressive stronghold. The city is home to vibrant African American, Latinx, and
Asian American communities. Residents voted for Obama by wide margins
in 2008 and 2012 and for Hillary Clinton in 2016. The city boasts distinc-
tive neighborhoods, a trendy downtown area, numerous breweries and art
galleries, and an affordable cost of living—all of which have helped Charlotte
attract a well-educated millennial workforce.

Charlotte is also split among nearly a dozen state legislative districts, and
its General Assembly delegation usually comprises mainly Democrats with a
handful of moderate Republicans. But in 2009, the 103rd District representing
the eastern part of the city elected William M. Brawley, a staunch conservative with a 100 percent rating from the American Conservative Union.[1]
Brawley's election moved the average ideology of Charlotte's state delegation
firmly to the right, and during his time in office Brawley voted to cut funding
to Medicaid and the North Carolina Department of Environmental Quality.

The year after Brawley was elected, the Charlotte City Council hired Dana Fenton, an advocate with decades of legislative affairs experience, to serve as the intergovernmental relations manager for the city. In this role, Fenton advises the city manager on intergovernmental policy issues, works with department heads to craft the city's legislative agenda, and lobbies the state government on measures that impact the city. The job keeps Fenton busy. Over the past decade, he's successfully maintained funding for Charlotte's light rail system and opposed bills that would have reduced the city's power to regulate local building standards. Currently, he's trying to build support for a proposal that would increase the city sales tax to fund a number of local transportation initiatives. "We've got some more work to do with our stakeholders before we can really move forward with that," he admitted. "It's likely going to be a 3–4 year effort."[2]

When and why do cities like Charlotte rely on professional advocates to represent them in their state governments? And why do cities lobby in certain years but not others? Was it a coincidence that Charlotte hired Fenton after its state legislative delegation shifted to the right, or might this reflect a more general logic employed by local officials trying to navigate the state-level political environment? In this chapter, I develop a theoretical framework to answer these questions and use the fifty-state lobbying data introduced in the previous chapter to test several implications of the theory.

As I discussed in Chapter 2, cities are generally quite transparent in their lobbying aims. They want to protect local revenue sources, fight back against state preemption, and encourage policies that increase local control. But it seems reasonable to assume that most cities share these goals. I argue that in order to understand why certain cities take the costly step of lobbying, we need to consider the relationship between city officials and their elected representatives in higher level office.

Local governments are fundamentally different from most other organizations that lobby because they are geographically nested in state and federal legislative districts. As a result, they receive a certain amount of de facto representation because elected officials in different levels of government represent the same constituents in the same physical space. I argue that when cities are able to rely directly on their elected officials in other levels of office to advocate for their preferred bundle of funding and policies, they should have less of an incentive to hire lobbyists. But when city leaders believe that their interests are not being adequately represented by their elected delegates in higher office, lobbying offers them an alternative channel through which to voice their needs. In other words, the quality of the vertical relationship between cities and their state representatives should contribute to the demand for lobbying. This argument expands on the logic of Payson (2020b), which focused more narrowly on how preference incongruence between cities and their state delegations leads to mobilization.

In this chapter, I begin by briefly surveying what we know about the determinants of lobbying from the interest group literature. Existing research suggests that municipal size and local economic resources should play a major role in the decision to lobby across cities. I then highlight how local governments are different from other interest groups and flesh out my theory of lobbying in the intergovernmental context. I also provide some initial qualitative evidence supporting the notion that the relationships between state and local officials influence municipal lobbying choices.

Next, I rely on the dataset introduced in Chapter 2 to formally demonstrate that cities are more likely to lobby when they face obstacles to effective representation by their state legislators. For example, city officials are more likely to hire lobbyists when they are redistricted in a way that increases the size of their delegation, as well as when they are mismatched with their state legislators in terms of partisanship and ideology. These findings highlight one of the important and often overlooked roles that lobbyists play in federal systems. If local governments aren't happy with the representation they receive directly from their elected officials, lobbyists can help amplify their message.

3.1 Why Do Organized Interests Lobby?

The interest group literature often focuses on two main determinants of lobbying: political stakes and organizational resources (Lowery and Brasher 2004; Grossmann 2013). Early studies of the governmental process by scholars like Truman (1951) and Dahl (1961) assumed that lobbying was a natural consequence of disturbances in the policy environment. According to this pluralistic perspective, groups mobilize when the stakes are sufficiently high, and the interests of society as a whole should be more or less represented through this process.

Researchers quickly realized, however, that policy concerns alone are not always sufficient to spark political action. This is particularly true when groups or individuals face incentives to free-ride off the advocacy efforts of others, which hinders the mobilization process and can lead to participatory bias (Olson 1965; Schattschneider 1960; Lowi 1969; Schlozman 1984; Salisbury 1984). But while pluralists and their critics disagree over the sufficient conditions for political activism, neither dispute the fact that organizations with more to gain (or lose) from government action have stronger incentives to lobby. The empirical literature offers ample support for this idea. For example, firms increase their lobbying activity when their industries are more heavily regulated (Stigler 1971; Hansen and Mitchell 2001), when they are more dependent on the government for sales and contracts (Tripathi 2000; Hart 2001), and when their business operations are more sensitive to potential government interventions (Salamon and Siegfried 1977; Grier, Munger, and Roberts 1994).

Both theory and evidence also suggest that organizations are more likely to become politically active when they have more resources at their disposal—including members, assets, and employees (Drope and Hansen 2006; Richter, Samphantharak, and Timmons 2009). The fact that resources are not equally distributed in society is precisely why scholars like Schattschneider rejected the pluralist notion that the lobbying process reflects the interests of the general public. Subsequent studies have confirmed that government policies tend to mirror the preferences of high-income citizens and economically powerful groups (e.g., Gilens 2012; Gilens and Page 2014). In short, while having skin in the game seems to be an important precondition for political activism, organizations with deep pockets or other types of political or economic capital are more likely to act on their interests by lobbying.

This work provides a useful starting point for thinking about why cities and other local governments might choose to lobby. Using the logic of stakes and resources, we would expect larger and more economically affluent cities to be the most active lobbyists. The stakes are clearly high for major metropolitan centers. Urban core cities have historically been both underrepresented in state legislatures and disproportionately impacted by state policy (Nice 1987; Gamm and Kousser 2010). Before the 1960s, state legislative districts were notoriously malapportioned, with city legislators representing twenty times more voters than non-urban lawmakers (Ansolabehere and Snyder 2008). Rural and suburban interests dominated, and state governments were viewed as "unsympathetic arenas" for urban concerns (Weir 1996, 24). Today, big cities tend to provide a variety of services to socioeconomically diverse populations and struggle to raise additional revenue without alienating their tax base (Peterson 1981). Securing adequate state funding is a constant priority, and the net result is that populous municipalities face particularly strong incentives to pay for lobbyist representation.[3]

At the same time, the interest group literature suggests that we should observe more lobbying by resource-rich cities, all else equal. From the perspective of local governments, the most important resource is generally a robust tax base from which to generate revenue. There are a variety of ways that the idea of city "wealth" might be operationalized—for example, median resident income, average housing values, or city revenue per capita. In practice, these indicators of local wealth often correlate with each other and tend to be concentrated in affluent suburban cities like Beverly Hills or Palo Alto. The resource hypothesis suggests that these communities should more easily be able to foot the bill for lobbying services. Local residents of these cities are also more likely to be politically attentive, which provides local officials with additional pressure to lobby (Verba, Schlozman, and Brady 1995).[4]

3.2 How Local Governments Are Different

While existing work on interest groups suggests several likely correlates of city lobbying, some important distinctions differentiate local governments from other types of institutions that lobby. One of the key differences is that local governments are particularly sensitive to their political geography. Cities are literally defined by their spatial boundaries. This stands in contrast to most membership-based groups or corporations, which tend to be regionally dispersed and geographically mobile. Businesses can relocate (or threaten to) if they are dissatisfied with the political environment in their district (e.g., Peterson 1981). Advocacy groups can target their efforts across multiple states and legislators to reach the most sympathetic audience. As a result, these types of interest organizations are better equipped to shop around the legislature for allies if they aren't happy with the actions of their district representatives.[5]

Cities, on the other hand, exercise little clout with lawmakers outside of their own districts. The votes of city residents have no impact on the electoral prospects of neighboring legislators, and cities are legally prohibited from contributing to political campaigns or forming PACS (Cammisa 1995). Jennifer Abele, the former in-house lobbyist from Milwaukee, told me that this was both a blessing and a curse from her perspective. "The disadvantage of being a public sector lobbyist or doing intergovernmental work is that you don't have a PAC behind you. You can't make any funding contributions to any politicians or causes. But I actually liked that. I didn't ever want to feel that I needed to put money behind someone in order in order to get a policy changed."[6]

The closest interest group analog to local governments might be other institutions that are fairly fixed in terms of their physical locations, like universities. In fact, De Figueiredo and Silverman (2006) find that the committee assignments of district congressional representatives matter a great deal for the lobbying behavior of universities. But in general, local officials are uniquely dependent on their elected delegations in other levels of government. As a former Washtenaw County Commissioner in Michigan observed, "We just don't have natural avenues for building strong relationships beyond the reach of our immediate delegation."[7] Those elected representatives in turn have reasons to pay special attention to the lobbying requests of local governments in their district because they represent the same constituents.

The argument in this chapter is that the quality of vertical representation should influence the demand for city lobbying. Literature in the American political development subfield has long recognized the historical importance of relationships between city officials and their state and federal delegations (Allard, Burns, and Gamm 1998; Burns et al. 2009; Gamm and Kousser 2013; Ogorzalek 2018). When these relationships work well, local officials can often get everything they need in terms of policy and funding without hiring lobbyists. Take the Bishop International Airport Authority in Flint, Michigan. Over the past few decades, the airport has secured millions of dollars in grant money to renovate and expand its facilities, and former airport director Jim Rice attributes this success entirely to the city's federal representatives. In particular, Rice singled out Rep. Dale Kildee (D-Flint), estimating that Kildee had garnered nearly $100 million in federal aid for the airport over the years via legislation and grant assistance. When asked by a local newspaper why the airport didn't pay for lobbyist representation, Rice mused: "We've just never really needed [lobbyists] . . . we've been successful enough using our senators and congressman."[8]

Former mayor Mike Houston of Springfield, Illinois, referred to this type of successful relationship between a city and its state delegation as "free" representation. Houston explained that rather than hiring a lobbyist, the city relies on its municipal officials and city council members to informally contact the district's state legislators.[9] In fact, many local officials pride themselves on developing strong relationships with their elected representatives, which they claim negates the need to employ lobbyists. This attitude is exemplified by the mayor of Kenai, Alaska, who asserted, "I've got a great relationship with all of our legislative delegation. I felt like local government shouldn't have to hire a lobbyist to lobby our legislators. We should go directly to them."[10] And the county mayor of Claiborne County, Tennessee, was even more explicit: "I am the lobbyist for Claiborne County. We don't need to be paying another one."[11]

Similarly, state and federal officials seem keenly aware of their special duty to represent the local governments in their district. Because this type of advocacy is such an important part of their job, some elected officials even express indignation when the governments in their district hire lobbyists. According to the chief of staff of Congressman Bill Young (R-Florida), "When asked the question whether a city or county needs to hire a lobbyist, he has always told them they don't need to hire a lobbyist to work with their own congressman. That's his job. Those are the people he was elected to represent. He doesn't need to work through somebody else to schedule a meeting with a mayor or a city council member."[12] State Representative Greg Davis of Minnesota explained that such behavior could even be interpreted as a snub. "It's insulting that [they] need to hire a lobbyist when we're elected to make sure our cities are in great shape."[13]

But while elected officials in higher office recognize their responsibility to represent local interests, not all local governments enjoy equally cozy relationships with their representatives. Sometimes, local officials might not be able to get the attention of their state and federal counterparts. City Manager Bryce Haderlie of West Jordan, Utah, claimed that one of the primary reasons his city sought out lobbyist representation was to "open doors of communication with legislators . . . that I just don't know how we would ever have access to."[14] Representatives might not be aware of local needs— or they might have spending and policy preferences that conflict with those of the local governments in their district. As Burns et al. (2009) bluntly observe, city delegations have "tremendous power to manage the state's involvement in city affairs. Some delegations wield this power effectively. Some do not." When local governments aren't getting what they want directly from their elected officeholders—whatever the reason—hiring lobbyists provides them with the opportunity to purchase additional advocacy in other levels of government.

In the previous chapter, I highlighted the primary channels through which lobbying might improve representational outcomes for cities. Lobbyists target both state legislators and the executive branch in an effort to secure beneficial policies, legislative earmarks, favorable regulations, and grants for their local clients. Lobbyists are also skilled at generating communication between state and local officeholders. A former county commissioner from Washtenaw County, Michigan, explained, "There's no shortage of weaving that happens. Our [lobbying firm] is particularly adept at this. I sit in probably two meetings a week with our lobbyist and a lawmaker. They see a large part of their role as facilitating conversations, and I think they do a pretty good job."[15]

A related part of this job involves alerting state representatives to local needs and persuading them to support city projects. For example, the city of Hartford, Connecticut, relies on its lobbyist to prepare reports and analysis detailing the local impacts of policies "so the city can say to the delegation 'Here's what you can do for us.'"[16] Dana Fenton of Charlotte added, "What I've found in my experience is that not all legislators really know what's going on inside the cities and counties they represent. What we do more than anything else is really just provide information about what's going on here in the city government."[17] Still other local officials say that they rely on lobbyists to signal urgency. A staff member from Diamond Bar, California, indicated that his city pursues a variety of strategies to advance its local agenda in the statehouse. "But for something that's urgent, then we get Gonsalves [our lobbyist] on the phone. It helps to convey the level of importance for an issue."[18]

The key assumption underlying my argument is simply that if cities could get what they wanted directly from their state representatives without paying for lobbyist advocacy, they would. Many mayors and city managers are in regular contact with their state legislators, and state lawmakers at least give lip service to the idea that their job is to represent their local governments in the statehouse. If local officials could pick up the phone and simply communicate their needs to their elected legislators for free, they should have less of an incentive to allocate scarce city revenue toward hiring lobbyists. This chapter examines several common representational challenges for cities and demonstrates that these scenarios consistently affect the lobbying decisions of local officials. The results are broadly consistent with a model of intergovernmental lobbying in which cities use lobbyists to compensate for the representational gaps that sometimes emerge in federal systems.

3.3 Predicting Lobbying across Cities

The analyses in the following sections combine the original data on city lobbying disclosures introduced in Chapter 2 with demographic data from the American Community Survey and financial data from the Census of Governments. The dataset also includes information about the lower chamber state legislators representing each city, drawn from Boris Shor and Nolan McCarty's American Legislatures project. The Shor and McCarty data identify the state representatives serving each district in a given year as well as a measure of their ideology, which they estimate by using survey responses and roll call votes.[19] In other words, lawmakers that tend to vote in favor of liberal legislation are assigned more liberal scores, while lawmakers that vote for conservative legislation are assigned conservative scores.

Recall that the lobbying data specifically document instances of *paid* lobbying, where municipal governments hire either internal lobbyists or external firms to represent their interests. To be clear, local officials can also "lobby" by communicating directly with their state representatives. As the anecdotes in the previous section suggest, this happens all the time. State house members typically spend up to half of each week in their districts attending meetings with local elected officials and constituents (Jewell 1982), and city mayors and council members often develop close relationships with their state delegation. While my measure of lobbying captures only the formal activities subject to state disclosure laws, the fact that informal communication also occurs between cities and their state members means that the reported results are likely an underestimate of the total lobbying that happens.[20]

I begin by looking at some descriptive patterns of city lobbying using the complete dataset, which consists of all municipalities with 5,000 residents or more between 2006 and 2015. Figure 3.1 shows the predicted probability of lobbying across several city characteristics after adjusting for a variety of other covariates in a pooled regression model.[21] For example, when comparing cities that are similar in terms of population, are cities with higher median incomes more likely to lobby? These variables were selected from a battery of financial and demographic indicators due to their predictive power, and I later use these them as control variables in the regression models that comprise the bulk of the analysis in this chapter.

As previewed in Chapter 2, there is a strong, positive correlation between city population and the likelihood of lobbying. Among the largest cities, the

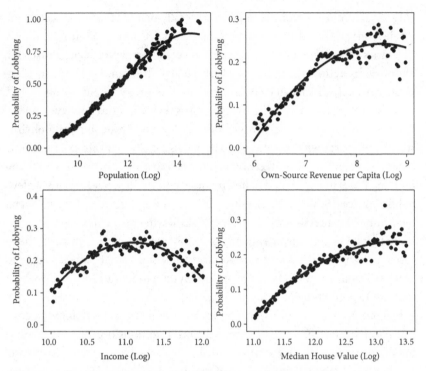

Figure 3.1 Correlates of Lobbying across Cities. Binned scatterplots showing predicted values across covariates from pooled OLS models.

probability of lobbying approaches 100 percent. This pattern is consistent with research on corporate influence and supports the political stakes hypothesis. Of the 100 most populous cities, 90 percent reported hiring lobbyists at some point between 2006 and 2015, with almost 60 percent lobbying every year. Perpetual city lobbyists include New York, Los Angeles, and Chicago, as well as Miami, Phoenix, and St. Louis. But many large cities reported lobbying in some years but not others, like San Francisco and Newark, and a few cities didn't disclose any lobbying activity during this period—including Boston.

The evidence for the resources hypothesis is slightly more mixed. On the one hand, both own-source revenue per capita and median housing values appear to correlate with lobbying. Own-source revenue is generated by cities locally, usually through property taxes, user fees and charges, and sometimes local sales taxes. But cities vary in their ability to raise local revenue, depending on property values and the affluence of the tax base. Cities that are able to raise more revenue locally are generally better-off economically and rely less on transfers from the state and federal government. Figure 3.1 shows that cities with more local, own-source revenue per capita at their disposal are more likely to hire lobbyists, all else equal. The same goes for median housing values, which can be considered another proxy for city wealth.

Interestingly, the median income of a city's residents does not have a linear relationship with lobbying across cities. Rather, the probability of lobbying steadily increases with income—and then falls for cities toward the top of the income distribution. This likely reflects the fact that some of the most affluent municipalities in the United States are quite small and provide relatively few public services. Some of these communities, like Atherton, California, were incorporated expressly with the purpose of allowing residents to control property taxes. Local governments might simply not be active enough in these cases to warrant hiring a dedicated lobbyist. These initial patterns suggest that city resources might be more important than individual resources when it comes to predicting lobbying across cities.

Of course, there are a variety of other local characteristics that might correlate with the decision to lobby, from the racial composition of a city to local unemployment rates. But it turns out that the variables depicted in Figure 3.1 do a good job explaining most of the variance. In fact, after accounting for city size and income, the share of white residents in a city has almost no relationship with the probability of lobbying (see Table A3.2 in the chapter appendix). Existing research indicates that racial diversity and especially racially segregation matter for outcomes like public service provision (e.g., Alesina, Baqir, and Easterly 1999; Hopkins 2009; Trounstine 2016), and there are many rich community dynamics that might increase or decrease the rate of city lobbying. But one of the goals of political science is to offer accounts of social phenomena that are as parsimonious as possible while still generating insight. From a prediction standpoint, the variables introduced here are among the most important for understanding city lobbying behavior.

These variables also mirror theoretical analogues in the interest group literature. But as I discussed in the previous section, the relationship between cities and their elected representatives should also influence the demand for lobbying. As a first step to examine this possibility, I introduce two representational variables as predictors: the number of lower house legislators representing a city, and the ideological distance between those lawmakers. Among cities in the sample, 40 percent have more than one elected legislator serving them, either because they sit in a multi-member district or because they are cut across multiple legislative districts. When city delegations comprise more than one representative, I define the ideological distance between them as the absolute value of the difference between the most conservative and the most liberal member.[22]

Figure 3.2 shows the predicted rate of lobbying across these two representational variables, again after adjusting for the covariates introduced in Figure 3.1. It appears that cities with larger delegations are more likely to lobby. This finding is consistent with the idea that coordinating across multiple representatives poses challenges for local officials. According to an intergovernmental affairs officer from Los Angeles, "We have the largest congressional delegation in D.C., and with that comes the need to maintain a continuous and ongoing engagement regarding priority legislative and administrative issues."[23] Communicating across districts requires additional time and energy on the part of municipal officials, and legislators may also face incentives to shift blame and unduly claim credit for state actions affecting their cities (Chen 2010). When cities are split across multiple districts, they also often share their representatives with other municipalities, which can divide the attention of the lawmaker. An employee of the Springfield Metro Sanitary District in Illinois explained, "We have multiple people [state representatives], but sometimes Springfield is on the fringe of a district. The actual district may be centered elsewhere. We feel it's better to have [lobbyist] representation, someone on your side if you have a particular issue."[24]

Figure 3.2 also suggests that the ideological distance between legislators is associated with an increased probability of city lobbying. In other words, when the delegates representing a city diverge ideologically, local leaders

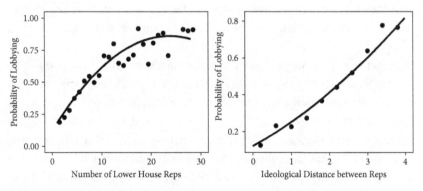

Figure 3.2 Representational Correlates of Lobbying. Binned scatterplots showing predicted values across covariates from pooled OLS models.

appear to be more likely to hire lobbyists. This finding complements a variety of historical work on the relationship between cities and their state legislative delegations. For example, Allard, Burns, and Gamm (1998) find that state legislators did not pass anti-urban legislation at particularly high rates—as long as the city delegation was unified in its opposition. But in the absence of such unity, Gamm and Kousser (2013) find that rural and suburban legislators dominate, and urban bills ultimately fail at higher rates. Burns et al. (2009) and Gamm and Kousser (2013) argue that this happens because disagreement among urban legislators muddles cues for others in the chamber. The larger the delegation, the greater the opportunity for internal division. In response, city officials hire lobbyists, perhaps with the hope of smoothing over these differences to ensure that their members present a unified front on local issues.

3.4 Too Much Representation? Redistricting and Lobbying

While the correlations established in the previous section are interesting, we can't yet draw causal conclusions about the relationship between representation and municipal lobbying. Cities with larger state delegations likely differ from those with fewer representatives in unobservable ways that might also influence their demand for lobbying—for example, they might be home to more politically active residents or provide more city services. A more convincing way to test whether larger delegations lead cities to lobby would be to examine the same cities over time as they gain or lose representatives. This approach holds constant underlying city characteristics that are time invariant, making it easier to isolate the effect of the number of representatives on lobbying.

In fact, many municipalities experienced just this situation after the 2010 census. State redistricting plans split 764 of the cities in the sample into additional districts, increasing the size of their delegations and providing an excellent natural experiment. When cities are redistricted so that more legislators represent them, are they more likely to lobby? I find that they are, on average. To draw this inference, I use an empirical setup where I examine the probability that cities lobby before and after being redistricted compared to other cities in the same state and year that didn't receive additional delegates.[25]

This approach reveals that gaining additional representatives increases the probability that a city hires a lobbyist by around 3.5 percentage points. While this effect might seem small, the average rate of lobbying across municipalities is only 16 percent in any given year. A 19.5 percent probability of lobbying thus reflects an increase of almost 20 percent from this baseline. When I replicate the analysis for big cities with populations over 100,000, I find even larger effects. Urban centers are around 9 percentage points more likely to hire lobbyists after being redistricted (see Table A3.3 in the chapter appendix).

Figure 3.3 shows the annual probability of lobbying before and after 2010 for the cities that were split across multiple districts compared to those that weren't. The data indicate that the cities that were redistricted to gain delegates noticeably increased their lobbying efforts starting around 2013. The first state elections using the new district boundaries tended to take place in 2012, with the new legislative session beginning in 2013, so it makes sense that this is when city leaders might choose to start lobbying.

Figure 3.3 also helps to rule out alternative causal stories about the relationship between lobbying and redistricting. For example, imagine that a city was rapidly gaining residents prior to 2010. That city might have been targeted by the state to be cut into multiple legislative districts to account

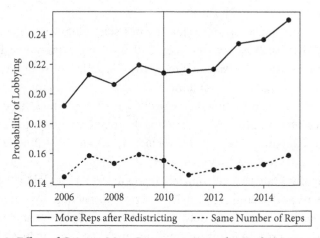

Figure 3.3 Effect of Gaining More Representatives after Redistricting on Lobbying. When cities are redistricted so that they are represented by more state legislators, they are more likely to lobby in the following years compared to cities that don't gain additional delegates.

for this population growth—but city leaders might have already started lobbying before the redistricting took place in order to meet the political demands of a growing community. In fact, the data demonstrate that the cities that were ultimately split into new districts did have a higher baseline rate of lobbying. But the *trends* in their lobbying behavior leading up to 2010 look nearly identical to the lobbying decisions of cities that didn't gain delegates. This suggests that municipal lobbying really was a response to being redistricted in a certain way, rather than being a cause of that redistricting in the first place.

One such city was South El Monte, California. Before 2010, South El Monte sat in the same legislative district as its sister cities, North El Monte and El Monte, all predominantly Latinx communities in the San Gabriel Valley. After redistricting, South El Monte was split across two state assembly districts, one of which crossed a mountain range and included several cities that were less racially diverse and more affluent. The city's mayor, Luis Aguinaga, explained that the new lines didn't make sense and that being divided from the neighboring towns would reduce the community's political clout in state government. "We're always on the same side, always fighting for the same issues. On this side of the San Gabriel Valley we have a voice. If we're apart it will be much harder to be heard."[26] After the 2011 election, South El Monte subsequently hired a lobbying firm, the Monares Group, to help communicate the city's legislative strategy to its new state delegation.

As an extension, I also examine if cities start lobbying when they are redistricted in such a way that they end up being represented by *fewer* legislators. In other words, is it simply the disruption of redistricting that increases lobbying, or is it something about the challenge of coordinating across more delegates? Using the same empirical setup, I find that cities that lose representatives through redistricting do not increase their probability of lobbying. If anything, they are slightly less likely to lobby—although the effect is small and not precisely estimated.

And finally, I find that city officials are no more likely to lobby the federal government after gaining state delegates via redistricting. Instead, they increase their lobbying efforts only at the state level. Rather than embarking on a full-court press in terms of mobilization, the decision to hire a lobbyist seems specifically aimed at addressing the more challenging representational dynamics that cities face in the statehouse after the size of their delegation increases.[27]

3.5 Partisan Mismatches and City Lobbying

The previous sections established some basic cross-sectional correlates of lobbying and then introduced a method to examine the lobbying decisions of the same cities over time in order to draw more robust inferences about the causes of this behavior. This approach revealed some initial evidence that the relationship between cities and their state legislators influences the demand for lobbying. The main argument in this chapter is that cities will choose to lobby when they face challenges to securing benefits directly from their district legislators. In this section, I consider two important representational dynamics that might make it more or less easy for cities to work with their elected delegates: shared partisanship and congruent ideology.

A well-established literature on distributive politics shows that local officials who share a partisan affiliation with their representatives in the central government tend to receive additional funding (Levitt and Snyder 1997; Solé-Ollé and Sorribas-Navarro 2008; Brollo and Nannicini 2012). There are a variety of reasons why partisanship might influence the relationship between local governments and their elected representatives in higher office. Members of the same party generally share a common network and enjoy more opportunities to meet and communicate, and they are also more likely to share policy goals and political preferences.

City officials frequently invoke partisan dynamics when describing their decision to lobby. According to Larry Ceisler, a lobbyist for the City of Philadelphia, "It's important that the city has a lobbying presence in Harrisburg, and it's doubly important that Philly, which is a Democratic city, has access to GOP leadership who basically run the show."[28] Interestingly, in-house city advocates echo this sentiment and sometimes rely on contract lobbyists to help them navigate particularly thorny political environments. After Republicans gained control of the Wisconsin State Legislature, Milwaukee's intergovernmental affairs director Jennifer Abele decided to pick up a contract with an external lobbying firm. "We chose a firm that had very heavy Republican connections," she told me. "Not necessarily to influence legislation, but just because we really felt like we needed insight into the political dynamics. Sometimes, I've found that if you can just get insight, it can help you prepare your arguments and responses. We relied on that team more for insight and monitoring than actual influence."[29]

Abele's experience helps make sense of an important puzzle. Why would legislators ever listen to lobbyists representing cities with conflicting views?

Local officials often claim that the goal of hiring professional lobbyists is simply to help them gain access to non co-partisan representatives. Many issues of great importance to local governments are complex and don't necessarily involve hot-button social issues. In these cases, information from local governments about the likely impacts of policies can still be useful to lawmakers from the opposite party—if the lawmakers are willing to have a discussion. Lobbyists can be very effective at facilitating these discussions, especially if state and local officeholders don't share a partisan network. As Rosenthal (1993) notes, "This style of lobbying tends to be straightforward and straitlaced and not overtly political."[30]

For example, Deece Eckstein, the lobbyist for blue-leaning Travis County, Texas, explained that he was able to work with the county's Republican delegation on a variety of issues with local fiscal implications. He explained that he "wasn't getting into the middle of abortion or constitutional carry."[31] Instead, his primary task was to provide reports and analysis to the county's Republican legislators to inform them about the local ramifications of potential state actions. His priorities in 2018 included convincing district lawmakers to oppose a property tax revenue cap on local governments and advocating for additional funding for county health clinics.[32] Similarly, Dana Fenton of Charlotte, North Carolina, said that one of his strategies for dealing with a Republican legislature was crafting a relatively narrow legislative agenda. "What we learned very early on when the Republicans took over ten years ago is that they believe the local governments had all the authority they needed, and therefore we basically shouldn't even bother asking for more than four or five things. We have pretty well stayed true to that, and we ended up with five objectives on our legislative agenda this year."[33]

To identify cases when cities face a partisan mismatch with their state representatives, I first need to classify cities according to their partisan leanings. Over 75 percent of municipalities in the United States have nonpartisan elections, making it difficult to assign partisanship based on the affiliation of the mayors or city council members. Instead, I rely on two proxies for city partisanship: the voting behavior of city residents in the 2008 presidential election, and estimates of city ideology generated by Tausanovitch and Warshaw (2014). While collecting reliable voting data at the city level is notoriously difficult in the United States (Marschall 2010), 2008 election returns are available for all cities with a population over 20,000 thanks to the efforts of Tausanovitch and Warshaw. The authors then constructed ideology scores for these cities by collecting hundreds of thousands of public opinion survey

responses from local residents about various political issues, which they
used to construct an overall index of city ideology ranging from very liberal
to very conservative.[34] The following analyses focus on the set of cities for
which these ideology scores are available.

I code municipalities as being either Democratic or Republican by binning
them into terciles based on their vote share for Obama in 2008 and their political ideology scores. I classify a city as Democratic if it falls in both the
top third of the Democratic vote share distribution and in the most liberal
third of the ideology scores established by Tausanovitch and Warshaw.[35]
Republican cities are those that fall in the bottom third of both distributions.
Figure 3.4 depicts this classification approach visually. The y-axis plots city
ideology (with higher scores reflecting more liberal policy preferences),
while the x-axis plots Democratic vote share in 2008. These two measures
correlate strongly. Perhaps unsurprisingly, the most liberal city in the sample
in terms of resident ideology is Berkeley, California. While urban voters tend

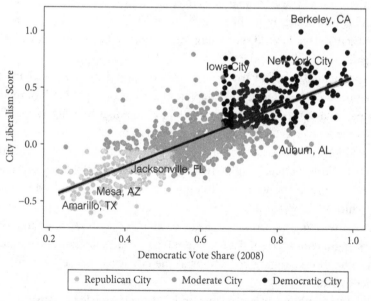

Figure 3.4 Classifying Republican and Democratic Cities. Cities falling in
the top third of presidential Democratic voteshare in 2008 or in the most
liberal third of the ideology scores established by Tausanovitch and Warshaw
are classified as Democratic. Cities in the bottom third of either measure are
classified as Republican.

blue, there are several large cities with more conservative tendencies, including Amarillo, Texas, and Mesa, Arizona.

I then map cities into their state legislative districts using geographic correspondence files from the Missouri Census Center. I define a partisan mismatch as occurring when a Democratic city is represented by a Republican state legislator or when a Republican city is represented by a Democratic state legislator. In the case of cities with multiple members, I code a mismatch as occurring when more than 50 percent of the delegation comes from the opposite party. As with the redistricting analysis, I exploit the fact that municipalities elect different types of representatives over time to estimate the effect of partisan mismatches on the probability of lobbying.[36]

In general, cities that vote blue tend to elect more Democratic representatives to the state legislature, and vice versa. But over the course of the panel, there were 538 elections that led to a switch in alignment between cities and their state delegation. The basic empirical strategy is to compare the change in lobbying probability for cities before and after their districts elect state legislators from the opposite party relative to cities that remain aligned. I further restrict these comparisons to cities in the same state and year—for example, how much more likely were cities to lobby in California in 2011 after their delegations flipped compared to other California cities whose delegations stayed the same?[37]

I also include control variables for the city-level demographic characteristics introduced earlier in this chapter, including total population, median income, own-source revenue per capita, and median housing values. This allows me to account for time-varying changes that might lead a city both to start lobbying and to elect a state representative from the opposite political party. For example, imagine that the median income of a city's residents was increasing in the years leading up to an election. Local leaders might opt to hire a lobbyist to advocate for a new set of state policies to help them address the changing economic needs of their residents. At the same time, voters might choose to support different types of state legislative candidates. Controlling for changing conditions at the city level can help me rule out stories like this.

Using this within-city approach, I find that an election leading to a partisan mismatch with the state delegation increases the probability of city lobbying by around 5 percentage points. The baseline lobbying probability for cities with populations over 20,000 is 48 percent, so 5 percentage points reflects around a 10 percent increase in the likelihood of disclosing lobbying activity.

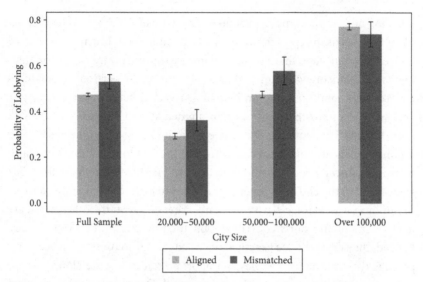

Figure 3.5 Effect of Delegation Mismatch on City Lobbying: Difference-in-Differences Predictions. When an election flips the partisan composition of a city's lower house delegation, small and mid-sized cities are more likely to lobby.

Figure 3.5 visualizes the change in the predicted probability of lobbying after a delegation mismatch occurs, broken down by city size. Complete results are shown in Tables A3.4 and A3.5 in the chapter appendix. As with the redistricting analysis, I also examine city lobbying behavior in the years leading up to the election that results in a partisan flip. I find no concerning trends that might indicate an issue with the research design.[38]

The cities that appear to be most sensitive to partisan mismatches tend to be small and mid-sized cities. Municipalities with populations between 20,000 and 100,000 are consistently more likely to hire lobbyists after their districts elect non co-partisans to represent them in the statehouse. Interestingly, urban centers with populations over 100,000 don't appear more likely to lobby at first blush. But recall that "lobbying" here is defined as the binary choice to hire a lobbyist or not. Large cities are already extremely likely to lobby, with nearly 80 percent reporting lobbying activity in a given year. Many of these cities employ full-time intergovernmental relations staff, which means they almost always engage in a baseline level of lobbying.

However, both Jennifer Abele and Dana Fenton told me that the cities of Milwaukee and Charlotte sometimes hire contract lobbyists to help out during particularly challenging legislative sessions. A binary measure of lobbying doesn't allow me to pick up on this type of dynamic. To further explore how partisan representation affects city lobbying, I turn to the subset of twenty-seven states that provide reliable expenditure information on their lobbying disclosure websites.[39] When I examine how partisan mismatches affect a city's total spending on lobbying, a very different picture emerges. Following elections that usher in non-aligned state delegations, cities with over 100,000 residents nearly *double* their lobbying expenditures.[40] This finding reveals an important distinction in the lobbying behavior of major metropolitan centers compared to small and mid-sized municipalities. For smaller cities, the choice is generally whether to pick up a lobbying contract or not in a particular legislative session. Larger cities, on the other hand, are likely to maintain a fairly consistent lobbying presence in their statehouses. Instead, they must choose exactly how much money to invest each year, and partisan dynamics appear to play an important role in this decision.

Next, I consider whether Republican and Democratic cities respond in similar ways to party mismatches with their delegations. Many of the examples provided throughout this chapter pit Democratic cities against their Republican legislators. But Republican cities also sometimes experience mismatches with their delegations. This often occurs when suburban municipalities reside in districts that also represent more racially diverse cities, often on the outskirts of urban core areas. For example, Citrus Heights, California, is significantly whiter and more conservative than many of its neighboring cities in Sacramento County. Its state assembly district leans purple, and in 2011 Richard Pan (D) was elected after Republican Roger Niello was termed out of office. Citrus Heights subsequently opted to hire a lobbyist, with the goal of securing state assistance for a new police service center and commercial revitalization efforts.[41]

Interestingly, I don't find major differences in the lobbying activity of Republican versus Democratic cities in response to partisan mismatches. On average, blue cities disclose lobbying activity at higher rates than red ones, and they are also more likely to be represented by members of the opposite party in the statehouse. But after an election flips the partisan composition of their delegations, both Republican and Democratic cities increase their probability of lobbying at similar rates. Figure 3.6 shows the predicted probability of lobbying broken down by city partisanship, and these results are presented formally in Table A3.7 in the chapter appendix.

In their research on cities lobbying the federal government, Goldstein and You (2017) find that Democratic cities in red states are much more likely to

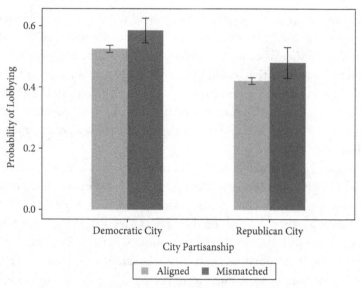

Figure 3.6 Effect of Delegation Mismatch on Lobbying by City
Partisanship: Difference-in-Differences Predictions. When an election flips the
partisan composition of a city's lower house delegation, both Republican and
Democratic cities mobilize at roughly equal rates.

lobby than Republican cities in blue states. They argue that this is because
liberal cities in Republican states typically prefer more spending on public
programs than their conservative state lawmakers are willing to fund. As a
result, they are forced to appeal to the federal government for aid. However,
it makes sense that such asymmetries might be less pronounced when it
comes to city officials lobbying in response to their relationships with their
district representatives, as both Republicans and Democrats actively work to
procure earmarks and funding for their own districts (e.g, Stein and Bickers
1994; Lazarus 2009).

3.6 The Unique Challenges
of Conservative Representation

The results in the previous section demonstrate that cities are more likely
to hire lobbyists when their districts elect representatives from the opposite political party. But is this because party networks make it more difficult to communicate with non co-partisans—or are local officials lobbying

because members of the opposing party hold divergent policy views that make it difficult for them to effectively represent city interests? Classic theoretical models often assume that the purpose of lobbying is to provide information to lawmakers that will help move their decisions closer to the ideal point of the interest group doing the lobbying (e.g., Potters and Van Winden 1992; Grossman and Helpman 2001). If this is the case, perhaps partisan mismatches between cities and state legislators are really a proxy for ideological distance.

To assess this possibility, I turn to the estimates of state legislator ideology provided by Shor and McCarty (2015) and previewed earlier in the chapter. Shor and McCarty assign ideology scores to legislators based on their responses to a national survey on their policy views as well as their roll call votes while in office.[42] Critically, this methodology allows Shor and McCarty to place lawmakers from different states on the same ideological scale. Higher scores indicate more conservative legislators, and lower scores indicate more liberal ones. Figure 3.7 depicts the ideological composition of the delegations of Republican and Democratic cities, broken down by the partisan mismatch variable used in the previous section. Unsurprisingly, Democratic cities tend to have more liberal delegations. But when Democratic cities elect mismatched delegations, the average representative ideology shifts noticeably to the right. The reverse is true for Republican cities: their district lawmakers tend to be fairly conservative, while their mismatched representatives fall more to the left.

When cities experience a partisan mismatch with their state delegation, are party dynamics driving the decision to lobby, or is it ideological divergence? Recall that I define a city as mismatched if more than 50 percent of its representatives come from the opposite political party. But as Figure 3.7 demonstrates, it's possible for majority Democratic delegations to lean moderate or even conservative, and vice versa for Republicans. I now examine how the probability of lobbying changes as cities elect representatives with more liberal (or conservative) ideologies, after accounting for legislator party.

Using the same empirical strategy as before, I compare changes in lobbying rates before and after the ideological composition of a city's delegation changes, relative to municipalities that don't experience such shifts. The regressions also include the partisan mismatch indicator as a predictor, allowing me to evaluate the marginal effect of ideology vis-à-vis party. Figure 3.8 shows these results. While the previous section demonstrated that the propensity to lobby increases about equally for Democratic and Republican

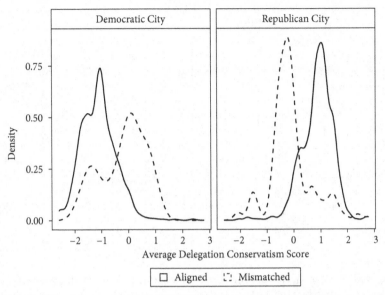

Figure 3.7 Delegation Ideology by Aligned and Mismatched Cities. Delegation conservatism scores are the average of the Shor and McCarty ideology scores for each legislator representing a city. Positive values are more conservative. Delegations representing Democratic cities are more ideologically liberal, and delegations representing Republican cities are more ideologically conservative. However, when an election flips the partisan composition of a city's delegation, the average ideology of the delegation shifts accordingly.

cities when members of the opposite party join their delegations, a very different picture emerges when looking at ideology. As state representatives move to the right, Democratic cities become dramatically more likely to hire lobbyists. But Republican cities are *also* modestly more likely to lobby as their delegations become more conservative.

In other words, staunchly conservative state representatives appear to pose special challenges to municipalities on both sides of the political spectrum. While liberal cities are especially allergic to conservative representation and increase their rate of lobbying significantly, red-leaning cities also disclose slightly more lobbying activity after their districts elect ultra-conservative delegations. Florida lobbyist Ron Book posits that, in the current political moment, conservative lawmakers often pose an existential threat to city autonomy. "Local governments are facing a state legislature where some lawmakers don't think they should be doing anything other than passing

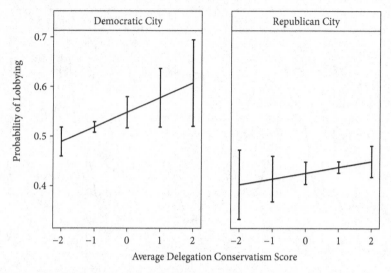

Figure 3.8 Effect of Delegation Conservatism on Lobbying: Difference-in-
Differences Predictions. Delegation conservatism scores are the average of the
Shor and McCarty ideology scores for each legislator representing a city. Positive
values are more conservative. After controlling for the partisan composition
of the delegation, Democratic cities are more likely to lobby as their delegate
ideology shifts to the right. However, Republican cities are also slightly more
likely to lobby as their delegations become more conservative.

Mothers' Day Resolutions," he told me. "So I do think the nature of that poses
unique challenges."[43] In Chapter 6, I explore in more detail how many of the
current policy battles in state politics involve cities lobbying their increasingly conservative state legislatures on matters related to local preemption.

3.7   District-Based or Collective Representation?
Evidence from Missouri

The findings presented so far indicate that cities are more likely to hire
lobbyists when they are represented by lower statehouse members from the
opposite political party. Both blue and red cities also lobby more as their
delegations become more ideologically conservative—although this effect
is particularly pronounced for Democrats. But how does the general ideological composition of the state legislature affect municipal lobbying? Are

cities lobbying primarily in response to ideological mismatches with their own representative, or does their alignment with the chamber as a whole also matter? To test this, I examine whether cities are more likely to disclose lobbying activity when lawmakers from the opposite political party gain control of their state legislatures.

There is some modest evidence that cities are more likely to hire lobbyists when members from the opposite party gain a majority in the legislature. These results are shown in Table A3.8 in the chapter appendix. The effect of a chamber mismatch is about half that of a mismatch with the city delegation, and it is also less precisely estimated. When accounting for both types of partisan dynamics, cities remain much more likely to lobby when their delegation flips relative to the chamber as a whole. This finding is largely consistent with the qualitative evidence presented earlier in the chapter. While the overall partisan composition of the legislature almost certainly matters for the representation of local interests, there is something special about the relationship between cities and their district delegation. City officeholders view their elected members as local representatives in the state legislature, and they often mention the role of their individual legislators in securing earmarks and other favorable policies for the district.[44]

If individual legislators are so important for city lobbying, we would expect to see municipal lobbying efforts geared primarily toward a city's district representatives rather than other members of the legislature. Although few states keep this type of information on file, Missouri is an exception. The Missouri secretary of state collects detailed information on all meetings between lobbyists and state officials, as well as the clients being represented. These data show that a majority of meetings between municipal lobbyists and legislators target a city's own elected officials. However, this rate is higher for small cities. Table 3.1 shows the percentage of city lobbyist meetings that are with a city's district representative, broken down by city size. Smaller municipalities like Branson, Centralia, and St. Peters contacted their own district legislators almost exclusively. Lobbyists for large cities like Kansas City and Springfield also met most often with local district lawmakers, but just under half of their meetings were with other state house legislators— typically senior members or chairs of important committees.

When thinking about the lobbying goals of local governments, it makes sense that cities would largely target their own representatives. These are elected officials that represent the same constituents, and the requests that local governments make directly affect the ability of state legislators to serve

Table 3.1 City Lobby Contacts in Missouri. While small cities contact their district representative almost exclusively, larger cities are more likely to contact other representatives as well as their own.

	N	% Lobbyist Contact with Own-District Rep.
Population <10,000	876	95
Population <75,000	65	78
Population 75,000+	8	52

their districts and eventually run for re-election. Historically, there is also some evidence that the most important step for cities hoping to secure particularistic policies from the state government was getting their state delegation on board. As Teaford (1984) wrote, "In state after state a favorable recommendation by the local delegation was virtually tantamount to passage" (91). And Allard, Burns, and Gamm (1998) found that almost all of the bills that would have affected big cities in the late nineteenth and early twentieth centuries were introduced by the representatives from those cities. The data from Missouri, though a bit speculative, lend some credence to the idea that local officials are, in fact, focusing their lobbying efforts on the representatives that serve their districts.

3.8 Discussion

This chapter sought to answer two questions. Why are certain cities more likely to hire lobbyists than others, and why do cities lobby in certain years and not others? Building off of my earlier work (Payson 2020b), I developed a simple theory of intergovernmental lobbying that emphasizes the role of political geography and the relationship between cities and their elected representatives in state office. I then tested several implications of this theory using the fifty-state lobbying data introduced in Chapter 2.

The interest group literature has consistently found that larger, more economically powerful groups are more likely to participate in politics. This chapter demonstrated that this is also true for local governments lobbying in the statehouse: cities with more residents, more own-source revenue, and higher property values are the most active lobbyists. But local governments

differ from other interest groups by virtue of their position within the f(
system. Because they are nested in legislative districts that are responsibl
representing local interests, cities are particularly attuned to their relationship with their state lawmakers when deciding whether to invest money in
lobbying.

The data indicate that a variety of representational scenarios affect municipal lobbying behavior. Local officials are more likely to hire lobbyists when
their cities are redistricted in a way that increases the size of their legislative
delegation. They also lobby when their districts elect members of the opposite political party to the state legislature, and Democratic cities are particularly likely to lobby as the ideological composition of their delegation shifts
to the right. For small and mid-sized cities, the primary decision is whether
to hire a lobbying firm or not in a given year. But for larger cities, the decision
often comes down to how much money to invest.

Qualitative and interview evidence suggests that there are several reasons
why lobbying might be beneficial for local leaders facing representational
obstacles. Lobbyists provide an alternative channel to voice local interests in
the legislature when a city's elected delegation has a different policy agenda.
Lobbyists can also facilitate meetings and communication between state
and local officials, which might be particularly useful in the absence of party
networks.

To be clear, I'm not arguing that redistricting or partisan mismatches are
the only or even the most important reasons why cities lobby. But representational dynamics like these are part of what make local governments unique
as interest groups, and they appear to matter a great deal for the lobbying
decisions of local officials. This chapter only begins to scratch the surface.
One of the goals of this research is to encourage scholars to continue theo-
rizing and studying the lobbying behavior of local governments.

For example, one city staffer that I spoke to in Diamond Bar, California,
observed, "There are some cities that are very intertwined with their elected
officials. Sometimes those jurisdictions will hire staffers that worked for their
elected officials, or their staffers will go and work for those elected officials
in state office. Anecdotally, it seems like these cities don't need a lobbying
firm."[45] Can political connections substitute for lobbyists in smaller cities?
What about when state lawmakers have previously worked for a city government? In this chapter, I focus on the lobbying behavior of cities, but other
local governments lobby as well. When surrounding counties and special
districts opt to hire lobbyists, are local governments able to work together to

achieve their goals—or does jurisdictional overlap lead to competition (e.g., Berry 2009)? These are just some of the questions that might make fruitful avenues for future research.

The results in this chapter highlight one of the potential benefits of intergovernmental lobbying. If local governments face obstacles to effective representation in state government, hiring a lobbyist can help bridge these representational gaps. But why is local government lobbying so much more common in some states than others? This is the question I turn to in the next chapter.

4

Exploring Municipal Mobilization
across States

We are a complicated legislature. [The local officials] just want to make sure that things are on track, and lobbyists can be helpful sometimes with that.

—Assembly Member Amy Paulin,
NY State Assembly District 88

Lobbyists help legislators, many of whom are inexperienced under term limits, cut through the static and get right to the important questions.

—City Council Member Bob Pacheco,
City of Walnut, CA

In June 1989, the Minnesota Office of the Legislative Auditor commissioned a study of local government lobbying in the state. The report found that lobbying expenditures by cities, counties, and school districts had increased sixfold since the 1970s and concluded that "at least some of the increase in lobbying is a response to conditions created by the Legislature. The property tax system and state funding formulas for local governments have grown more complex, and local dependence on the state has increased. Also, the Legislature has often been responsive to lobbying efforts."[1] And yet, while local government lobbying is common in states like Minnesota, in other parts of the country very few individual cities hire lobbyists to formally represent them in their state capitols.

The previous chapter analyzed how different local factors influence the lobbying decisions of city officials. But there are also stark differences across states in the overall propensity of local governments to rely on lobbyists for representation. Figure 4.1 maps the fraction of cities lobbying in each state visually.[2] On average, states can expect around 16 percent of their municipalities to disclose lobbying activity in a given year, but this rate is much higher in places like Florida, Nevada, and Washington. Why do states vary so dramatically in the proportion of cities that choose to lobby? And which state-level conditions are associated with local government mobilization? These are the questions I address in this chapter.

I begin by briefly reviewing what we know about differences in the lobbying environments across states. Most interest group scholarship has focused on explaining patterns of lobbying behavior and campaign contributions at the federal level, while only a few foundational studies engage with questions of state-level mobilization, including Gray and Lowery (1996), Thomas and Hrebenar (2004), and Rosenthal (1993). Drawing from this literature and my own research, I introduce three categories of contextual variables—geographic, institutional, and political—that I hypothesize might influence municipal lobbying intensity.

Unfortunately, few of the geographic or institutional factors associated with intergovernmental lobbying are time-varying at the state level over the course of the available panel data, which runs from 2006 to 2015 for the majority of states.[3] This means that most of the following analyses

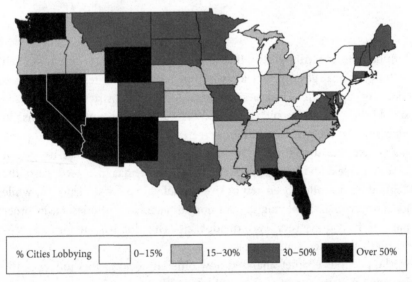

Figure 4.1 Proportion of Cities Lobbying by State. A higher percentage of cities lobby in the West, while Northeastern states experience lobbying by a lower proportion of municipalities.

are limited to cross-sectional description rather than causal identification. Nevertheless, they provide some initial insight as to why municipal lobbying rates vary so widely across states and suggest avenues for further research. After establishing these cross-state patterns, I examine the correlates of city lobbying within each state for the set of variables that vary over time.

It turns out that many of the political dynamics that correlate with municipal lobbying across states fail to explain within-state mobilization. An important exception is the level of city reliance on state transfers for revenue, which fluctuates from budget cycle to budget cycle. I uncover evidence that more cities within a state lobby when state transfers comprise a larger share of city budgets—but this relationship works in the opposite direction, too. Levels of municipal lobbying also appear to influence the distribution of state revenue to cities in the first place. I drill down on this finding and examine the funding and policy consequences of municipal lobbying in the next two chapters.

Finally, I discuss several recent state efforts to ban or regulate intergovernmental lobbying. While these efforts have so far gained little traction, they help shed light on some of the normative concerns surrounding lobbying by local officials. Arguments in favor of such restrictions typically emphasize the cost to taxpayers and raise questions about the appropriateness of using public funds to try to influence government policy. But as I discuss in the final chapter of the book, it's unclear how targeting local government lobbying in this way would improve democratic policymaking in the absence of broader structural reforms to the lobbying industry.

4.1 What We Know about Variation in State-Level Lobbying

In Chapter 2, I described why collecting data on state-level lobbying is more challenging than at the federal level because each state employs its own lobby disclosure laws and reporting systems. However, a few studies have attempted to examine interest mobilization across states, generally relying on qualitative evidence and cross-sectional surveys. Hrebenar and Thomas (1987; 1993a; 1993b) and Rosenthal (1993) provide rich descriptive accounts of who state lobbyists are, what tactics they use, and the policy battles that ensue. Subsequent work by Gray and Lowery (1996) draws from population ecology models in biology to develop a theoretical account of why interest

s vary in their size and impact across states based on the distri-
~~sources.

These authors demonstrate that interest group activity in the states expanded dramatically in the 1980s as states began actively legislating on environmental standards, the workplace, consumer affairs, and other types of
social issues. Devolution and deregulation by the federal government left
states in charge of important policy areas, and interest groups responded
by shifting their advocacy efforts away from DC and toward state capitols.
However, it was often difficult for this early research to draw systematic
conclusions about the role of particular state-level conditions on aggregate
lobbying behavior. As Thomas and Hrebenar (2004) write, "Although there
are some common influences across the states, the impact of groups in a
particular state is a product of the unique ways in which these influences
interact and change. . . . Thus, although some common denominators do
exist across the states, changes in single group power, overall interest power,
and group system power often depend on the individual circumstances in a
state" (137).

While the circumstances of individual states undoubtedly shape interest
group mobilization in important ways, the literature on state politics and
policy also suggests several common variables that might help to explain
the intensity of local government lobbying. These include both institutional
arrangements—such as the presence of term limits and the level of professionalization in a state legislature—and political dynamics, like the party in
control of state government and the degree of polarization. I discuss the theoretical predictions for each of these variables in more detail in the following
sections. But first, I examine how several basic features of state geography
contribute to city lobbying rates.

4.2 Political Geography and Municipal Lobbying

As I argued in Chapter 3, one of the characteristics of local governments that
makes them unique as interest groups is their political geography. Cities are
defined by physical boundaries and embedded in a multilevel system of government in which their vertical relationships with elected officials in higher
office matter a great deal. It makes sense that the spatial composition of cities
and their residents across a state might also influence the overall demand for
lobbying by local officials.

I examine the correlation between overall rates of city lobbying and two geographic variables: degree of urbanization and municipal density. I define the degree of urbanization as the average city population in a state. How big are cities in that state, on average? The previous chapters uncovered evidence that the number of residents in a city is the single strongest predictor of whether a municipality discloses lobbying activity or not. If a state tends to have larger cities, we would expect that a higher proportion of those cities would lobby compared to states with smaller, less populous municipalities.

The level of municipal density within a state refers to the number of cities divided by the state's land area. In some states, like California and Texas, city clusters are relatively spread out, while in others, like New Jersey, large numbers of municipalities cover a smaller geographic area. When individual cities hire lobbyists, they often do so with the hope of securing particularistic benefits. However, in densely populated states, a high degree of spillover often exists in terms of public goods provision across municipalities. Anecdotal evidence suggests that cities in these states tend to rely more heavily on the advocacy efforts of their municipal leagues or on coalitions of neighboring cities, rather than lobbying on their own.

Figure 4.2 shows the predicted percentage of cities lobbying across these two geographic variables from pooled regression models that are described in more detail in the chapter appendix. Because the proportion of cities lobbying within a state is sensitive to the total number of municipalities, I always control for this in each of the following analyses. The average city size in a state has a clear, positive relationship with the percentage of cities lobbying

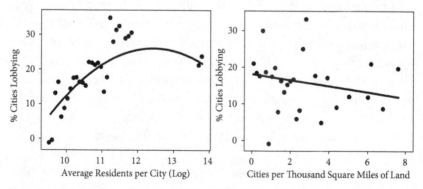

Figure 4.2 Geographic Correlates of City Lobbying across States. Binned scatterplots showing predicted values across covariates from pooled OLS models.

in that state. Recall that the cities appearing in my sample are those with an average population of at least 5,000 residents. Some states, like Nevada, have relatively few incorporated cities above this threshold, but those cities are relatively populous. The fact that states with larger cities experience a greater degree of overall municipal lobbying follows directly from the fact that larger cities face stronger incentives to lobby, as described in Chapter 3.

There also appears to be a modest negative correlation between municipal density within a state and the percentage of cities lobbying. The densest state, New Jersey, has 194 cities with at least 5,000 residents and a land area of 7,400 square miles. Instead of hiring individual lobbyists, New Jersey cities tend to rely heavily on the New Jersey League of Municipalities to represent their interests. In fact, the New Jersey League of Municipalities is one of the most active municipal leagues of any state. In 2017, it ranked 31 out of 943 registered lobbying organizations in New Jersey in terms of its expenditures, placing it in the top 3 percent of spenders. Given the close geographic proximity of New Jersey municipalities across the state, it makes sense that cities might pool their lobbying efforts through municipal leagues rather than hiring individual lobbyists.

4.3 Lobbying in Response to Institutional Complexity

Having established two basic geographic correlates of city lobbying across states, I turn to several institutional variables that might also influence the propensity of local governments to lobby. The first is the presence of local property tax limitations, which restrict the ability of cities to raise local revenue. Forty-six states impose some form of property tax limitation that dictates the rate at which local governments can increase taxes on homeowners. States began adopting these laws in the 1970s as part of the "taxpayer revolt" that ushered in the Reagan Era.[4] California's Proposition 13 marked one early victory for proponents of these measures. This ballot initiative amended the state constitution to cap the maximum ad valorem tax rate on real property at 1 percent of the cash value and paved the way for similar efforts in other states.

There are three broad categories of property tax limits. Assessment limitations restrict the rate at which property taxes can be increased as a result of growth in assessed property value. Rate limits cap the overall ad valorem tax rate that can be set by elected officials. And levy restrictions limit the overall amount of revenue that a government can collect from property taxes.[5] States often use a mix of these strategies, with twelve states imposing one type of limit, twenty-five states imposing two, and eight states imposing all three categories of local property tax limitations.

What are local officials to do when faced with such constraints on their ability to raise revenue locally? One option available to them is to hire lobbyists to seek out other sources of funding via earmarks, grants, and state appropriations. As I discussed in Chapter 2, trying to secure additional revenue for their clients is one of the major goals of city lobbyists. City officeholders also lobby the state legislature to approve changes to their local taxation rates. Dana Fenton, the intergovernmental relations manager of Charlotte, North Carolina, explained that many of his recent advocacy efforts have centered on building support for a proposed increase to the local sales tax, which the General Assembly would need to explicitly approve.[6] Figure 4.3 depicts the percentage of cities lobbying by state broken down by the number of property tax limitations in place. The more limits a state has on the books, the higher the percentage of its cities that opt to lobby.

It's important to note that this association between local tax limitations and city lobbying may or may not indicate a causal relationship. For example, perhaps state officials chose to adopt these laws in places where city lobbying was already common. But lobbyists that have represented cities for decades—like Anthony Gonsalves of California—told me that the caps

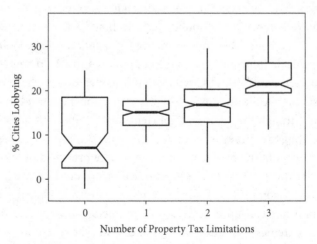

Figure 4.3 Local Tax Limits and City Lobbying across States. A higher proportion of cities lobby in states with stricter local tax limits.

came first, followed by a growing demand for lobbying services among local governments. Gonsalves explained, "There were 107 cities in the state of California that were less than 7 percent share of the property tax, and there were 31 that had no share of the property tax. When we started representing those small cities—this was after Prop 13 and after AB 8—we were finding that these cities had actually no voice in Sacramento before we started representing them."[7]

Next, I examine the relationship between aggregate city lobbying and two institutional features widely studied in the literature: term limits and state legislative professionalism. Term limits are generally found to increase lobbying efforts across interest groups of all types (Cain and Levin 1999; Carey and Powell 2000; Moncrief and Thompson 2001). This happens because increased turnover among legislators leads lawmakers to rely more heavily on the institutional knowledge and expertise of lobbyists and other outside groups. According to Frank McNulty, the former speaker of the Colorado House of Representatives, "Term limits really started to come into effect in the early 2000s, and the legislators that had been serving a long time and the committee chairs started to cycle out. That caused a growth in the lobbying industry. In state legislatures, more so than in Congress, you have more rapid turnover of the key opinion leaders. So if you're a good lobbyist on the state level, you're constantly investing in these new relationships."[8]

Classic theories of lobbying emphasize that one of the important roles of lobbyists is to subsidize the legislative efforts of elected lawmakers by helping to research and craft policy (e.g., Hall and Deardorff 2006). When term limits increase the turnover among legislators in office, lobbyists can provide valuable information about local interests that help new legislators get up to speed. As Walnut City Council Member Bob Pacheco observed, "Lobbyists help legislators, many of whom are inexperienced under term limits, cut through the static and get right to the important questions."[9] In fact, according to a survey of new members of the California state legislature, over 90 percent of the bills they introduced were proposed or even drafted by lobbyists during their first year in office (Cain and Kousser 2004). The former county commissioner for Washtenaw County, Michigan, added that state term limits end up devolving may problems down to the local level. "That puts a tremendous burden on us financially," he said. "In the House of Representatives, they flip out on average every four years. It creates a patchwork of implementation."[10]

While there are theoretical reasons to believe that state term limits will increase local government lobbying, the role of legislative professionalism is a bit less clear. Scholars generally define legislative professionalism as "the capacity of the [legislature] to generate and digest information in the policymaking process" (Squire 2007). In the 1960s, Alexander Heard described legislatures of earlier eras as "poorly organized; technically ill equipped; functioning with inadequate time, staff, and space; and operating with outmoded procedures and committee systems" (1966, 3). But over the next few decades, legislative reform movements swept through many states, with the goal of professionalizing and reshaping state legislatures to more closely resemble the US Congress. During this time, state legislatures increased member pay and extended the length of their legislative sessions. The number of legislative staffers doubled in most states between 1968 and 1974 and increased another 25 percent between 1979 and 1988 (Rosenthal 1993).

Reformers hoped that these efforts would attract better candidates to state office and improve policy outcomes. Today, scholars generally measure legislative professionalism via the Squire Index (1992; 2007). This index evaluates state legislatures on a variety of dimensions—including the length of the legislative session, the number of full-time staff, and member salaries—and then assigns scores based on how closely the institution mirrors Congress. Higher scores indicate greater professionalization, and scores range from a low of 0.027 (New Hampshire) to a high of 0.626 (California).

Legislative professionalism has been demonstrated to affect a great many political phenomena, including the relationship between campaign contribution limits and polarization (Barber 2016), the level of policy responsiveness (Lax and Phillips 2009), variation in representational style (Maestas 2000; Harden 2013), and rates of policy innovation and diffusion (Tolbert, Mossberger, and McNeal 2008). But there are competing theoretical predictions about whether and how professionalization contributes to interest group mobilization. On the one hand, more professional legislatures might rely less on lobbyists if the resources at their disposal make it easier for them to secure information via their staff members (Berkman 2001). At the same time, more professionalized legislatures tend to deal with more complex informational environments and to process a greater number of bills (Bowling and Ferguson 2001)—which might allow interest groups to exert greater influence.

Local officials frequently invoke state governmental complexity as a key reason why they choose to hire legislative advocates. A lobbyist for Patricia

Lynch Associates in New York State described how "new mandates—like the property tax freeze—pose tremendous challenges for local governments. Government is more complicated than ever, and local officials—many of whom are part-time—really do need help."[11] The mayor of Sandy, Utah, echoed this sentiment. "Cities lack the sophistication needed to effectively deal with the state legislature and Congress that have become much more complex. You need professional help."[12]

Interestingly, it turns out that neither term limits nor legislative professionalism alone can account for overall municipal lobbying rates across states. Instead, cities disclose more lobbying activity in states with both term limits *and* highly professionalized legislatures. Figure 4.4 shows this relationship visually. Legislative professionalism correlates positively with city lobbying in term-limited states but negatively in non-term-limited states. The combination of legislative complexity along with regular turnover among members seems to predict substantial rates of city mobilization. Results from regression models including each of the geographic and institutional variables above can be found in the chapter appendix.

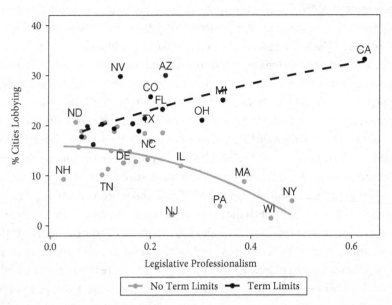

Figure 4.4 State Legislative Professionalism, Term Limits, and City Lobbying. A higher proportion of cities lobby in states with both more professional legislatures and term limits.

However, these conditions might spur lobbying by all interest groups in a state—not just local governments. To assess whether any of these state-level variables correlate specifically with municipal mobilization (rather than lobbying more generally), I use data from Lowery et al. (2012) that provide information about the distribution of registered lobbyists across interest group categories in 2007. On average, cities comprised just under 2 percent of all registered interest groups across states, although in California they made up over 7 percent.

It turns out, the combination of term limits and legislative professionalism not only predicts overall city lobbying rates, but these institutional features also correlate with cities comprising a larger share of the overall interest group community. One possible explanation for this finding is that in more professionalized legislatures without term limits, long-serving state delegations can develop strong relationship with the local governments in their district that negate the need for lobbyists. Weir, Wolman, and Swanstrom (2005) found that in Michigan and Ohio, long-standing personal ties between cities and their delegations were the norm prior to term limits. In less professionalized legislatures, where lawmakers debate many fewer bills each session, these relationships between local and state leaders might simply not matter as much.

Yet again, these correlations may or may not indicate any sort of causal relationship between these state-level institutions and the lobbying behavior of cities. California, a state with term limits and a highly professionalized legislature, differs from other states in numerous ways—both observable and unobservable—and it could be these underlying conditions that led state lawmakers to adopt these particular institutions while simultaneously incentivizing local governments to hire lobbyists. But given how little we know about why city mobilization rates vary across states, establishing these initial patterns is a crucial step to develop theory and advance this research agenda.

4.4 The Political Environment

The previous section demonstrated that cities tend to lobby more in complex information environments with high turnover rates among lawmakers. This result highlights one of the potential upsides of municipal lobbying. Namely, local lobbying can provide valuable information to legislators about local needs amid complicated and constantly changing institutional

landscapes. Intergovernmental lobbying may well facilitate legislative efficiency when lawmakers are less certain about the best way to represent their
local constituents.

I now examine several political variables that might increase or decrease
the overall rate of lobbying by cities across states. These include the party
of the governor, the partisan composition of the legislature, whether a state
is experiencing divided government, and the level of polarization between
Republican and Democratic lawmakers. The data for the following analyses
come from the Correlates of State Policy Project (Caughey and Warshaw
2016; Jordan and Grossmann 2020).

Relationships between cities and state governors have historically been
marked by confrontation. During the Progressive Era, governors would
sometimes send in the state militia to enforce gambling and liquor laws in
large cities (Berman 2003). Governors often vocally support tax and spending
regimes that strip away power and funding from specific localities—
particularly governors elected from the Republican Party. Governors also actively shape the distribution of government aid across their states and exert
substantial control over the budgeting process. If Republican governors are
more likely to embrace austerity than Democratic ones, then this might lead
more cities in those states to hire lobbyists.

Similarly, the party composition of the legislature likely changes the
lobbying calculus of local officials. In Chapter 3, I demonstrated that individual cities are more likely to lobby when their district is represented by
a state legislator from the opposite political party. Similar dynamics may
or may not show up in the aggregate. If Republican cities hire lobbyists
when Democrats sweep into office—and vice versa—the overall rate of city
lobbying might look similar across party regimes, even if comprised of different cities.

However, qualitative evidence suggests that Republican control of the legislature might pose a special challenge to cities. Surveys of mayors reveal that
while both Democrat and Republican mayors grumble about the levels of
funding they receive from their states, Democratic mayors in Republican
states express particular dissatisfaction (Einstein and Glick 2017). State municipal leagues have also experienced growing tension with "the pocket of
resistance they have found from ultra-conservative or libertarian legislators
on the Republican side who see municipal leagues or leagues of cities as
closely tied to unacceptable big government or progressive causes and the
Democratic Party" (Berman 2003). Given that cities tend to lean more to

the left than rural areas, municipal officials may be especially likely t
when Republicans control the state legislature.

Divided government may or may not correlate with municipal lobbying
rates. On the one hand, when different parties control the legislature and
governorship, the associated budgetary conflicts might increase interest
group mobilization (Clarke 1998). At the same time, the gridlock associated
with divided government might mean that local officials see lobbying as a
waste of time and resources. In fact, one of the widely articulated hypotheses
for why lobbying activity has surged at the state level since the 1990s is because interest groups recognized the extreme difficulty of passing legislation
in a divided and gridlocked Congress.

Finally, I examine the relationship between partisan polarization and the
proportion of cities lobbying. Gray et al. (2015) find that the level of party
polarization in a state's legislature is positively associated with the rate of interest mobilization—but only for nonprofit and public sector organizations.
For other types of groups, the number of registered lobbyists stays fairly
constant regardless of polarization. They theorize that the uncertainty and
competition associated with polarization might be particularly salient for
public organizations with ties to party networks. To examine this possibility,
I examine how the average ideological distance between Republicans and
Democrats in the state legislature correlates with city lobbying. These ideological distance measures are generated via the Shor and McCarty (2015)
data on state legislator roll call votes introduced in the previous chapter.

Figure 4.5 shows the estimated coefficients from a pooled regression
model with year fixed effects. The year fixed effects help to account for variation in municipal lobbying that might be driven by year-specific shocks, such
as the financial crisis in 2008. Full regression results are in the chapter appendix. *Republican Governor* and *Divided Government* are dummy variables
that take a value of either zero or one. The *% of House Republicans* ranges
from zero to one hundred, and *Polarization* ranges from 0.467 to 3.746.

Each of these variables is positively associated with municipal lobbying
rates across states. The proportion of cities hiring a lobbyist is 2.5 percentage
points higher in states with Republican governors and with divided government. The relationship between city mobilization and Republican presence
in the legislature is a bit noisier, but it appears that a greater proportion of
cities lobby in states with a higher proportion of Republican lawmakers.
Polarization also has a strong, positive correlation with local lobbying. A 1-
point increase in the polarization rate (around 30% of the scale) is associated

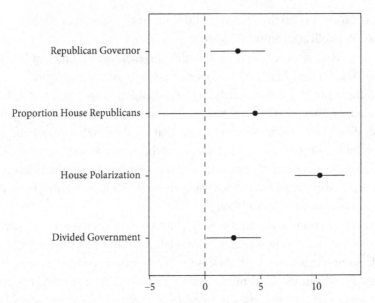

Figure 4.5 Political Correlates of City Lobbying. Coefficients with 95% confidence intervals from pooled OLS models.

with a nearly 10 percentage point increase in the proportion of cities that report hiring lobbyists.

Throughout this chapter, I've cautioned against assigning causal stories to the correlational results suggested by the data. We just don't know if these political dynamics cause cities to mobilize, or if the lobbying behavior of cities contributes to the state political environment, or if some other state-level factor is responsible for both outcomes. However, unlike the geographic and institutional variables introduced in the previous sections, these political characteristics changed over time within many states during the course of the panel. As a result, I can perform a within-state analysis that examines how changes in the partisan composition of the state government correlate with changes in city lobbying activity. In other words, after accounting for time-invariant, state-specific conditions that might affect the overall rate of municipal lobbying, how does the election of a Republican governor or an increase in legislative polarization influence city mobilization behavior?

In order for this approach to yield insight, the overall rate of municipal lobbying needs to vary over time within states. Figure A4.1 in the chapter appendix depicts the proportion of cities that disclosed lobbying activity each year, broken down by state. Some states, like Wisconsin, West Virginia, and

Pennsylvania, experience very low rates of city mobilization across years, while other states experience more fluctuation. The average proportion of cities lobbying changes by around 2–5 percentage points from year to year in most states.

Interestingly, after restricting the analysis within state, the estimated relationship between municipal lobbying and each of the variables shown in Figure 4.5 disappears. The one coefficient that continues to approach statistical significance is the level of polarization in the legislature—but the coefficient now points in the opposite direction, indicating that as polarization increases within a state, the proportion of cities lobbying actually *decreases*.[13] This analysis perfectly illustrates the limitations of relying on cross-sectional data to draw causal inferences. When we look across states, legislative polarization appears to correlate with municipal lobbying. But this doesn't mean that polarization necessarily causes this behavior. Rather, the political dynamics in highly polarized states likely differ from those in less polarized states along a number of dimensions—including, for example, the level of legislative gridlock and the divergence in preferences of urban versus rural delegations. We can't conclude definitively which of these dynamics leads cities to mobilize at higher rates.

However, there is one political variable that continues to demonstrate a strong, positive relationship with city lobbying even after performing this within-state analysis. Both across and within states, I find that city officials are more likely to disclose lobbying activity when they rely more heavily on the state for revenue. Across the United States, cities receive anywhere from 2 to 80 percent of their revenue from the state, but this varies from place to place. In Connecticut, the average city gets 36 percent of its revenue from the state government, while in West Virginia, this amount hovers closer to 3 percent. However, state budgets and revenue sources vary dramatically from year to year based on macroeconomic factors. When I include state transfers as a share of the average city budget as a predictor variable, both the cross-sectional and within-state regressions yield large, positive estimates.

4.5 State Transfers to Cities Increases Lobbying—And Vice Versa

Figure 4.6 shows the relationship between city reliance on state transfers and overall rates of city lobbying both across and within states. The figure on the left shows that as state transfers comprise a greater share of city budgets, a higher proportion of cities hire lobbyists. The figure on the right shows this relationship after demeaning both variables by state and year. In other words, after accounting for average differences in transfer levels across states and across particular years, how much does a *change* in city reliance on transfers influence the proportion of cities that choose to hire lobbyists?

For every 5 percentage point increase in the share of state transfers comprising the average city budget, municipal lobbying rates increase by around 2 percentage points in that state. The state budgeting process therefore seems to matter a great deal for the lobbying decisions of local officials. It makes sense that more cities might choose to engage in lobbying when their ability to operate and provide services depends more heavily on state funding. Lobbyists claim that one of their most critical jobs is helping cities to protect their existing sources of revenue. If that revenue comes from the state, that's where city lobbyists will focus their efforts. Explained Jeff Coyle, the inter-governmental affairs liaison for San Antonio, Texas, "We spend 80 percent of our time playing defense, working to protect existing levels of state funding rather than lobbying for new legislation."[14]

But while it seems logical for more cities to lobby in response to demand created by the state budgeting process, might these lobbying efforts in turn shape that distribution process to begin with? To examine this possibility, I introduce leads and lags of the state dependency variable to assess how this relationship evolves over time. In fact, it turns out that city lobbying efforts

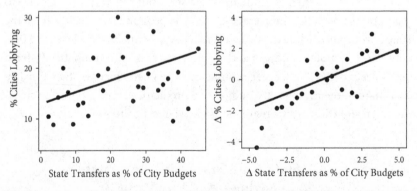

Figure 4.6 State Transfers and City Lobbying across and within States. Binned scatterplots showing predicted rates of city lobbying. The figure on the left shows this variation across states, while the figure on the right shows the relationship between transfers and lobbying demeaned by state and by year.

also appear to increase the share of state revenue allocated to cities in the first place. Figure 4.7 shows the relationship between the percent of cities lobbying within a state in various years and the proportion of the average city budget comprised of state transfers.

The data suggest that in states where transfers make up a smaller percentage of city budgets, cities start to mobilize—which then increases overall state funding to cities. In turn, this dependency creates a cycle and increases the rate of municipal lobbying. In Chapters 5 and 6, I delve more systematically into the question of what cities actually get when they lobby and how this behavior shapes state policy and funding outcomes. But the initial evidence presented in Figure 4.7 points to an important relationship that exists between state budget cycles and the mobilization choices of local officials.

4.6 Current Policy Debates

State courts have consistently upheld the right of local governments to hire lobbyists (Fernandes 2009). The 1927 case *Crawford v. Imperial Irrigation*

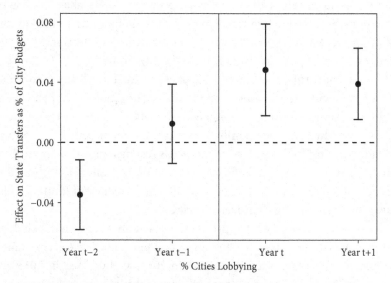

Figure 4.7 Within-State Effect of Lobbying on State Transfers as a Proportion of City Budgets. State fixed effects models show that as the proportion of cities lobbying increases, so does city reliance on state transfers.

District marked one of the earliest opportunities for the courts to weigh in on the question of local government lobbying. D. R. Crawford was a taxpayer in Imperial County, California, who sued his local irrigation district for using public funds to pay for a lobbyist. However, the California Supreme Court ultimately ruled that local governments possess the right to "contract for advocacy services."[15] While courts have generally been permissive of local government lobbying, they have ruled that local governments can't form or donate to PACs or spend public money on campaign contributions (Morgan 1984). But as Berman (2003) points out, legal precedents have been a bit vague in clarifying the conceptual differences between local governments lobbying versus engaging in other electoral activities. In recent years, there have been a growing number of lawsuits that seek to challenge the ability of governments to lobby with public money—particularly in southern states.

Public concern over "taxpayer-funded lobbying" flared in 2007, when Americans for Prosperity member Peggy Venable won a lawsuit filed against Williamson County, Texas, and the Texas Association of Counties. As Chapter 2 explained, most local governments in the United States lobby at least indirectly by paying dues to government associations. Venable sued her county on the grounds that it had used general revenue funds to lobby—which was in violation of state laws. According to Venable, "Taxpayers should not be forced to finance lobbying activities. Taxpayer-funded groups lobby for more of our tax dollars and oppose taxpayer protections. It is a vicious cycle, and it's fiscally, morally, and ethically wrong."[16]

But the court ruling in the Venable case provided the Texas Association of Counties with an easy workaround. The organization could continue to lobby if it simply separated its lobbying budget from its general revenue funds. And while one county initially rescinded its membership from the association during the lawsuit, county officials resumed paying dues once the lawsuit had concluded.[17] The Texas Association of Counties continued to lobby, and the case ultimately demonstrated the difficulty of limiting intergovernmental lobbying from a legal perspective.

Some states have tried to introduce legislation that would ban local governments from lobbying, but most of these efforts have also failed. Oklahoma considered such a measure in 2014, as did Texas in 2015 and Florida in 2017—but none of these bills made it to the floor. Arizona governor Doug Ducey did successfully issue an executive order in 2016 that prevented state government entities from hiring lobbyists. However, this order only applied to state agencies, boards, and commissions, and not local governments.

Supporters of these efforts typically claim that local government lobbying wastes public money and that taxpayers should not be forced to finance lobbying activities that they might not agree with. Many elected officials agree, claiming that voters shouldn't have to pay for politicians to talk to one another. "It's a disgrace that taxpayer dollars are used to hire lobbyists when we elect people to represent them," opined Florida House Rep. Richard Corcoran (R-Land O'Lakes).[18] Others point to potential equity concerns and question whether local governments enjoy equal access to lobbyist representation. Jack Gould, the chairman of Common Cause Nebraska, specifically cites the case of school districts. "You've got 17 school districts that can afford to hire lobbyists, and you've got 240-some that can't," Gould said. "They can barely hire teachers."[19]

However, it is far from clear that taxpayers would save money if governments were to stop hiring professional lobbyists. When cities and other local governments employ full-time staff members to lobby on their behalf, this work is also paid for by taxpayers. Costs also exist if local elected officials are the ones directly engaged in advocacy. Such efforts take away time from other responsibilities, and local politicians may or may not be effective at communicating their needs to higher levels of government. "The average [local elected official] has no idea how to lobby," explained Victor Crist, the county commissioner of Hillsborough, Florida. "You've got to have a full-time person monitoring the process, engaged in the process and developing relationships."[20] Bennet Sandlin of the Texas Municipal League echoed this sentiment, adding, "Mayors are busy filling potholes and putting out fires. It's unrealistic to expect a mayor to keep up with 6,500 bills filed during a regular session."[21]

Ultimately, the effects of initiatives to ban intergovernmental lobbying depend on what types of substitute behaviors are available. As long as incentives to shape state policy exist, local governments will find ways to exert influence—in all likelihood by working around various disclosure loopholes. For example, many states define a lobbyist as someone who spends more than 20 percent of her time advocating on behalf of clients. If a city employed someone who spent only 15 percent of her time lobbying on behalf of the local government, it would not be required to disclose that information in many states. Practically speaking, the vast majority of efforts to ban local government lobbying have failed to gain traction over the past decade, and such action does not appear to be likely in the near future. I return to the question of potential policy implications and possibilities for reform in the book's conclusion.

4.7 Discussion

While local factors like city population, economic resources, and relationships with state officials shape the lobbying calculus of local officials, the state-level environment matters as well. States with larger, more spread-out cities experience higher rates of lobbying than states with smaller, more densely located municipalities. Even more strikingly, states with term limits and more complex, professionalized legislatures observe substantially more municipal lobbying than other states. These two institutional variables further predict local governments comprising a larger proportion of all registered interest groups in a state.

While the political dynamics of state government also appear to correlate with local government mobilization, it turns out that these relationships are likely driven by other circumstances specific to a given state. The party in control of the governorship and legislature explains little of the within-state variation in the lobbying decisions of local officials. However, cities do appear to respond to the level of state funding available in a given year and adjust their lobbying behavior accordingly. More cities lobby when a greater share of their budget is comprised of state transfers—and these lobbying efforts in turn seem to increase state funding to cities.

In general, identifying the environmental factors that predict lobbying is challenging. Many of these contextual variables don't vary over time during the period for which data are available, which rules out the possibility of using panel methods to draw causal inferences about the effects of changes in state policies on lobbying. Future work in this area will likely benefit from historical case studies and more detailed, within-state analyses on the emergence of the local government lobby.

States have generally not restricted intergovernmental lobbying through formal policy channels—although some opponents have sought to limit "taxpayer-funded" lobbying via both legal and legislative means. While these efforts have proven largely unsuccessful so far, changes to the regulation of local government lobbying would provide a unique opportunity to evaluate the effects of state intervention on lobbying behavior. The next chapter shifts gears from seeking to explain when and why local officials mobilize and turns to the question of funding and policy consequences.

5

Who Gets What? City Lobbying and
State Transfers

For $6 a person, if [the lobbyist] is successful in getting us that
$125,000 in planning and design for this community center, that's a
real good return on investment.

—Mayor Dave Hill,
Algona, Washington

But after three years, $220,000 and half a dozen requests for money,
all Lake Mary got was a $100,000 clock tower that plays Christmas
and wedding music. So the City Council terminated the contract last
year, then promptly hired another lobbyist, based in Orlando.

—"Hiring Lobbyists, Towns Learn Money Talks,"
New York Times

Between 2008 and 2018, Utah experienced the highest percentage population growth of any state in the country.[1] Local officials attributed this influx of residents to the state's affordable cost of living, natural beauty, and sustained commitment to the public university system. Lured by the business-friendly environment, tech and startup companies flocked to the metropolitan area surrounding Salt Lake City, earning it the nickname "Silicon Slopes." As the region grew, the state also invested heavily in infrastructure and public transit developments, making hundreds of millions of dollars available to fund highway projects, expand light rail service, and build a new commuter rail system.

City officials quickly scrambled to secure this additional funding. West Jordan was among the communities jostling for more state money as it sought to widen a stretch of highway leading to the South Valley Regional

Airport. But Mayor Kim Rolfe was disappointed with initial efforts and voiced concern that other cities seemed to be having more luck—particularly those that hired lobbyists. "I must state that a couple of neighbors to our east have five different firms that represent them and spend over $500,000," Rolfe said. "If you look specifically at the transportation funding and some of the other funding that comes from the state, even though they're much smaller than us, they get a lot larger share of those because of the lobbyists that work for them."[2]

In response, West Jordan hired its own lobbying firm, Foxley & Pignanelli, which promised to help secure permits to locate an auto mall in the city, gain voter approval for a proposed sales tax increase, and identify funding for local transportation projects. Sure enough, in the next legislative session, West Jordan received an appropriation of $1,100,000 for highway improvements.[3] Mayor Rolfe was delighted, claiming that the expense of hiring the firm was well worth the cost and that the lobbyists were "worth their weight in gold."[4]

The first half of this book was primarily concerned with understanding the conditions under which local officials choose to lobby. In this chapter, it's time to start thinking about consequences. Qualitative evidence and interviews suggest that local officials share the same basic interests when it comes to influencing the state. They want funding and favorable policies that increase their power, autonomy, and institutional flexibility. Some cities are represented by state officials that proactively help them to achieve these goals; others turn to lobbyists to advocate on their behalf in the statehouse. But what do cities actually *get* when they lobby? Is spending money on intergovernmental lobbying a good investment? If it is, what types of cities tend to benefit the most?

Not surprisingly, lobbyists claim that their services are lucrative for their local government clients. Townsend Public Affairs, a prominent local government lobbying firm in California, boasts on its website: "We are proud to have won millions of dollars in state funding for our clients for projects such as parks, schools, roadways, rail lines, museums, historic buildings, public transit, libraries, water infrastructure, housing developments, and open space."[5] Other firms emphasize their ability to help cities maintain existing levels of state revenue or claim that without their professional help, local officials might easily end up with an unfunded mandate or canceled project financing. Dana Fenton, the in-house lobbyist for Charlotte, North Carolina, told me that soon after accepting his position for the city, the state threatened to strike funding for the city's light rail system. Fenton recounted, "In the first year of the process, the state senate tried to remove all the state funding for that project from the budget, and that would have killed the project. We were eventually able to reach a compromise, and luckily the amount of money that was agreed upon each year was the bare minimum we needed to keep the project going."[6]

Local political officials tend to talk about hiring lobbyists in terms of an economic investment. Robert Doyle, the general manager of the East Bay Regional Park District in California, estimates that his district has earned roughly $10 for every dollar spent on lobbying over the years. State funding that he attributes to lobbying includes a $13 million wildlife conservation grant and a new fire truck for the district's firefighting unit. "That's a pretty good investment," mused Doyle.[7] The mayor of Treasure Island, Florida, agreed with this assessment, citing a variety of earmarks that the city's lobbying firm has helped generate over the years and concluding, "They're worth every penny they get."[8]

But if lobbying is so effective, this introduces a puzzle. Why don't all local governments pay for lobbying services? Ansolabehere, De Figueiredo, and Snyder (2003) posed a classic formulation of this question in their influential paper "Why Is There So Little Money in U.S. Politics?" Building on work by Tullock (1972), Ansolabehere and his coauthors reason that if political contributions could really "buy" policy, we would expect donors to spend much more money trying to influence politics than they actually do given the billions of dollars in public expenditures at stake. They go on to argue that campaign contributions should be thought of less as a policy investment and more like a form of consumption that allows individuals and groups to engage with the political process by expressing their views.

In this chapter, I offer a slightly different answer to this puzzle as it relates to local government behavior. I provide evidence that hiring lobbyists does— on average—increase the revenue that cities receive from the state. But this is not true for every city in every legislative session. Given the high variance in outcomes, I argue that time and budget constrained local officials view lobbying more as a gamble than a safe economic investment. And while the data suggest that the expected returns to lobbying are positive over the long run, local politicians often face short-term pressures to produce results. Add competing policy priorities and different levels of risk tolerance to the mix, and it makes sense that cities might not always lobby despite the potential for positive benefits.

The main empirical challenge to estimating the returns
cities is that the decision to hire a lobbyist is far from random
siderations almost certainly influence how local government
decision of whether to lobby or not. On the one hand, cities mig
they are eligible for certain programs or expect that they wou   ...... good
candidates for funding. This type of self-selection would likely introduce up-
ward bias to the estimated effects of lobbying. On the other hand, cities might
lobby as a last-ditch effort when they are desperate for funding and have no
other options. In Chapter 3, I uncovered at least some evidence consistent
with this latter story. Cities tend to lobby more when they face various representational obstacles, which suggests that local officials use lobbyists when
they expect to receive less favorable treatment from the state. This type of selection would lead me to underestimate the true impact of lobbying.

Throughout this chapter, I present a variety of both qualitative and data-
driven evidence to assess the likely direction of unobservable selection bias.
Reassuringly, there appears to be a largely idiosyncratic component to the
lobbying decisions of many local officials. Cities lobby for lots of reasons
under circumstances that are more or less advantageous. Ultimately, the
patterns uncovered from an observational study like this one are still infor-
mative given that, in practice, lobbying is never actually randomly assigned
across cities.

Finally, I turn to the question of whether certain communities tend to benefit more from lobbying than others. One of the most pressing debates in
research on interest groups asks whether particular types of interests are able
to bias the political system in their favor. Schattschneider (1960) famously
articulated a version of this concern in *The Semisovereign People*, quipping
that "the flaw in the pluralist heaven is that the heavenly chorus sings with
a strong upper-class accent" (35). Indeed, a variety of empirical evidence
demonstrates that government policies tend to mirror the preferences of
high-income citizens and economically powerful groups (e.g., Gilens 2012;
Gilens and Page 2014). In earlier work, I demonstrate that cities with more
own-source revenue available to them netted higher state transfers after
lobbying in California (Payson 2020a). Do affluent communities enjoy a systematic advantage when it comes to lobbying across the country?

If lobbying does tend to be more effective for wealthy municipalities, this
would help to address one of the long-standing puzzles in the fiscal federalism
literature, which is that state transfers are often less progressive than theory
would predict (Oates 1972). Many states claim that their transfer systems are

designed to reduce regional inequality. The stated goal of New York's revenue sharing program, for example, is to "redistribute tax dollars broadly to municipalities which do not have the tax base or taxing authority to generate this revenue on their own."[9] And yet, intergovernmental transfers often do little to mitigate local inequality and sometimes even exacerbate it (Peterson 1995; Rodríguez-Pose and Ezcurra 2009). One possible reason for this discrepancy is that economically powerful local actors can manipulate the distribution of state funds through lobbying.

To assess if this is the case, I examine how the effect of lobbying varies by local income level. Rather than equalizing funding across cities, I find that lobbying disproportionately benefits places with high-income residents. These results provide some of the first evidence that intergovernmental lobbying might play a role in perpetuating revenue inequality across local governments by influencing the distribution of state funds. The rest of the chapter considers various explanations for this pattern and discusses how these findings complicate some of the initial conclusions drawn in the first half of the book. While intergovernmental lobbying can sometimes serve as a corrective to the vertical representational gaps that emerge in multilevel government, this ability to pay for representation can also favor certain local interests over others.

5.1 Is Lobbying a Good Investment for Cities?

Political scientists have grappled with the question of what interest groups get when they lobby for decades. Early models of lobbying assumed the process was essentially an economic transaction, with groups "purchasing" favorable policies via lobbying and other forms of political spending (Tullock 1967; Stigler 1971; Denzau and Munger 1986). But for many years, empirical evidence gave little indication that money bought legislative votes (Wright 1985; Grenzke 1989; Ansolabehere, De Figueiredo, and Snyder 2003; Baumgartner et al. 2012). As Baumgartner and Leech (1998) summarized, "The unavoidable conclusion is that PACs and direct lobbying sometimes strongly influence congressional voting, sometimes have marginal influence, and sometimes fail to exert influence" (134).[10]

Given these initial null results, political scientists developed new theories to explain the purpose of lobbying in other ways. Hall and Wayman (1990) offered a theory emphasizing the role of access and the ability of lobbying to buy time and attention from legislators. A large class of informational models emerged that consider how lobbying enables groups with particular subject-matter knowledge to transmit that information to generalist legislators lacking in expertise (Austen-Smith 1993; Potters and Van Winden 1992; Grossman and Helpman 2001). Still other scholars have argued that lobbying is primarily a form of legislative subsidy that allows lobbyists to help facilitate lawmaking (Hall and Deardorff 2006).

But recent work on corporate lobbying demonstrates that organizations may, in fact, profit economically when they hire lobbyists. For example, Richter, Samphantharak, and Timmons (2009) find that companies enjoy lower effective tax rates the year after lobbying. Alexander, Mazza, and Scholz (2009) use corporate tax disclosures on earnings from the American Jobs Creation Act of 2004 to show that firms lobbying for the provision received a return of $220 for every $1 spent. And De Figueiredo and Silverman (2006) estimate the returns to lobbying by universities, demonstrating that lobbying increases legislative earmarks. De Figueiredo and Richter (2014) provide an excellent review of the recent empirical work on lobbying. Together, these findings suggest that lobbying may have an economic logic that was not captured by earlier studies.

On average, I expect municipal lobbying to generate positive returns for cities. After all, it would be difficult to explain why cities hire lobbyists if there weren't the possibility of a successful outcome. However, I also argue that substantial uncertainty exists over exactly what cities will get in exchange for purchasing these services and how successful their lobbying efforts will be. Local officials in Hanford, California, know this all too well. In 2014, the Hanford City Council decided to cancel its contract with CrisCom, a small lobbying firm in Southern California, overriding the advice of the city's police chief. The city was trying to secure funding for a new police station, but several council members expressed impatience with the lack of results. However, in the following year, it wasn't Hanford but the neighboring city of Corcoran that ended up snagging over $3 million in public safety funding—by using the services of CrisCom. The Hanford police chief subsequently lamented, "It's a little like gambling. You just don't know if you're going to get anything or not."[11]

The analogy of gambling offers a useful way to think about the decision facing local governments. Imagine city officials have some baseline expectation about how much funding they will receive from the state or how friendly the state's policy agenda will be toward local interests. They might decide they are happy with this baseline. Or, they might conclude that they could get a better deal by hiring a lobbyist. As I discussed in Chapter 2, lobbyists pursue a variety of strategies that might help cities secure state benefits. They lobby for and against legislation with local impacts and advocate in favor of appropriations and earmarks. They identify grants that their clients are eligible for and work to shape the regulatory environment. However, city officials can't know for sure that these efforts will be successful. There is some probability that lobbying will be a good investment—but there is no guarantee. In fact, cities regularly switch lobbying firms or even stop lobbying altogether because they decide the costs don't actually outweigh the benefits.

So when might cities choose to "gamble" by taking the costly step of hiring a lobbyist? On the one hand, they might do this when they believe their status quo prospects are sufficiently bleak that any increase in the likelihood of securing funding or favorable policy would be very attractive. As we've seen in previous chapters, this seems to be the case for large cities facing persistent anti-urban bias in state legislatures as well as for cities that diverge from their state delegation in terms of policy and funding preferences. On the other hand, cities might lobby if the anticipated payoff is sufficiently high relative to the cost, or if they have good reasons to believe that their efforts will be successful. This would explain why we observe more lobbying by cities with more local resources at their disposal, who can more easily afford the risk. Similarly, the results in Chapter 4 indicated that cities are also more likely to lobby when state transfers comprise a larger share of municipal budgets— that is, when the stakes are high.

Overall, this framework offers a rationale for why some cities might not hire lobbyists even if municipal lobbying generates positive returns, on average. If city leaders have budget constraints and different levels of risk tolerance, it makes sense that not all cities would choose to lobby, even if the expected value of doing so is positive in the long run.

5.2 Using State Transfers to Estimate the Returns to Lobbying

In the following analyses, I focus specifically on how the decision to hire a lobbyist influences subsequent state transfers to cities. There are several advantages to using this particular outcome measure. First, both city officials and local lobbyists claim that securing state funding is one of the primary goals of investing in lobbyist representation. Of course, cities also lobby for a variety of other reasons. They want to be involved with crafting the state policies that will affect them, and they sometimes lobby defensively against unfunded mandates or to block legislation that would encroach on local control. But as I demonstrated in Chapter 2, one of the stated or implicit objectives of municipal lobbying efforts almost always includes increasing revenue from the state.

The lobbyists that I spoke to shared many examples of policy victories that they achieved for their cities, some of which centered on state funding and others which didn't. Jason and Anthony Gonsalves successfully helped the City of Cerritos, California, negotiate a settlement with the California Department of Finance to reclaim outstanding loan balances that the city would have lost after the state dissolved its redevelopment agency in 2011. Jennifer Abele, the in-house lobbyist for Milwaukee, worked with the state legislature to change the funding formula for public schools and estimates that the new formula has saved Milwaukee taxpayers over $100 million. And Florida lobbyist Ron Book described his efforts working with the City of Miami to secure authority from the state to impose a local parking tax.

While all of these examples are interesting, it would also be impossible to collect such fine-grained details on lobbying outcomes for each of the cities in my sample. In fact, previous studies of lobbying that focus on policy content and passage rates typically uncover null effects (e.g., Hojnacki et al. 2012), suggesting that such qualitative measures are too nuanced to make effective dependent variables. Instead, I draw on data from the Census and Survey of Local Government Finances to examine how lobbying influences net state transfers to cities. State transfers offer a clear, continuous outcome that allows me to compare the lobbying successes of thousands of cities across multiple states and years. While this approach may not capture all of the complex and interesting ways in which lobbying matters for cities, it provides an important starting point for this research agenda.

Unfortunately, the Census of Governments does not disclose the origin of the state transfer, so we don't know whether the additional revenue is coming from legislative earmarks, executive grants, or other sources. Based on the qualitative evidence, it appears that lobbyists pursue funding from each of these channels, although legislative lobbying is by far the most common. The goal of this chapter is not to isolate the precise mechanism linking lobbying to transfers. Rather, it's to establish whether such a relationship exists in the first place and to learn more about the types of places that tend to benefit.

Further decomposing the causal mechanisms that drive the results is a topic ripe for future research.

I employ the same basic empirical strategy in this chapter that I've used throughout the book. Armed with panel data on cities over time, I can exploit the temporal nature of local lobbying choices and estimate the within-city effect of lobbying on state transfers. That is, how much money do cities get before and after they lobby, relative to what other cities are getting and relative to their own yearly averages?

However, while I have access to annual data on city lobbying and demographics, the Census of Governments does not provide financial data for every city in every year. Instead, a complete census is taken in years ending in 2 or 7, and data are provided for a sample of municipalities in the intervening years via the annual Survey of Local Government Finances. On average, most cities appear in my dataset six times between 2006 and 2015.[12] But 15 percent of municipalities only appear twice, in 2007 and 2012. At the same time, cities with a population above 20,000 are sampled every year, and nearly 20 percent of the cities in my dataset have complete financial data available over the ten-year period.

I rely on this subset of cities with annual financial data to perform several robustness checks, including inspecting the pre-treatment trends of lobbying and non-lobbying cities. Are the places that opt to hire lobbyists experiencing financial distress (or an economic windfall) prior to their decision to lobby? If so, any change in state transfers might reflect these changes in underlying conditions rather than indicating that the city lobbying efforts were successful. Of course, the cities with complete financial data provided by the Survey of Local Government Finances tend to be larger than municipalities that only appear a few times in the sample. To further probe whether the within-city research design appears sound, I replicate this analysis using a set of three states—California, Florida, and Washington—that collect their own municipal revenue data independently of the Survey of Local Governments.[13] Using both datasets, I find that cities consistently net more state revenue after lobbying and no evidence of concerning trends leading up to this decision.

Next, I turn to the question of heterogeneous effects. Are the returns to lobbying evenly distributed, or do certain cities tend to benefit disproportionately? There are both theoretical and empirical reasons to believe that more affluent cities might enjoy an advantage when it comes to lobbying. To test this, I allow the effect of lobbying to vary by local income. I find that wealthier municipalities consistently get more state revenue after disclosing lobbying activity than their poorer counterparts. The chapter concludes by considering several explanations for this pattern and discussing some of the implications for public policy.

5.3 Lobbying Increases State Funding

I begin by inspecting the raw data to examine whether a correlation exists between lobbying and state transfers cross-sectionally. Figure 5.1 plots the density distribution of per capita state transfers for lobbying and non-lobbying cities. Lobbying cities do receive slightly more money from the state, on average, although there is substantial overlap in the distributions. More formally, I estimate pooled regressions where I model state transfers per capita as an outcome with a variety of predictors, including lobbying status, population, median income, own-source revenue, percent white, and median housing values. I also include state and year fixed effects to account

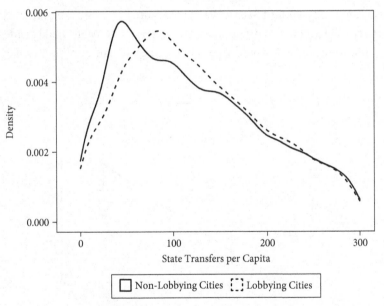

Figure 5.1 Lobbying and State Transfers across Cities. Cross-sectionally, lobbying cities tend to receive more state transfers per capita than non-lobbying cities.

for state-level differences and year-specific shocks in the amount of revenue cities receive from the state. These results are shown in Table A5.1 in the chapter appendix. After adjusting for these characteristics, lobbying cities continue to net around $23 more per capita than their non-lobbying counterparts.

As I've emphasized throughout the book, this correlation may or may not indicate that lobbying *causes* an increase in state transfers. Despite the battery of control variables, unobservable factors may well contribute to the lobbying decisions of local officials while also influencing the state funding a city receives. Perhaps places that provide more municipal services or that elect entrepreneurial city council members are more likely to hire lobbyists— but these places might receive more state revenue for reasons unrelated to lobbying. By focusing my analysis within city (rather than across city), I can adjust for any such influences that are time-invariant. While time-varying confounders are still a concern, which I discuss in the next section, the within-city approach helps to paint a more credible causal story.

Over the course of the panel, 1,044 cities disclosed lobbying activity in certain years but not others. When I compare cities that start lobbying to those that don't in the same state and year, the data indicate that lobbying increases state funding by around $10 per capita.[14] Figure 5.2 shows the predicted effect of hiring a lobbyist visually. For an average-sized city of 38,000 residents, this bump in revenue would translate into nearly half a million dollars of

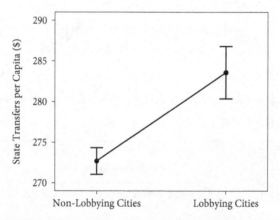

Figure 5.2 Lobbying and State Transfers: Difference-in-Differences Predictions. Compared to other cities in the same state and year, cities that lobby get more state funding than those that don't.

additional funding. While not a huge windfall, the average municipality in the sample spent around this amount on welfare each year between 2006 and 2015. And of course, some cities receive a much larger influx of funding after lobbying.

I also examine how the effect of lobbying varies by city size. Mid-sized cities with between 50,000 and 100,000 residents enjoy the highest returns, netting an additional $19 per capita after picking up a lobbying contract. But municipalities of all sizes do well when they lobby. Urban centers with over 100,000 residents get $12 per capita, and smaller cities with fewer than 50,000 generate $7 per capita in returns. Drilling down into the data, mid-sized municipalities are precisely the ones that are most likely to start and stop lobbying over the course of the panel, which means they provide a key source of variation for the research design. For example, if the largest metropolitan cities engage in lobbying activity every year, the empirical strategy I'm using can't identify how *changes* in their lobbying status affect their funding.

As a placebo test, I also check if lobbying the federal government increases state funding. If federal lobbying were to have a positive effect on state transfers, this would raise concerns. After all, lobbying the federal government shouldn't impact how much revenue a city gets from the state—unless some sort of change in local conditions was leading local officials to lobby both levels of government while simultaneously influencing municipal funding. For example, if a city was suffering from an economic downturn, local officials might lobby both levels of government out of desperation for additional revenue—but the city might also secure additional state funding simply by being eligible for more assistance. Reassuringly, the data show that lobbying the federal government has no effect on state transfers. And even after adjusting for federal lobbying, the binary decision to lobby the state continues to have a robust, positive relationship with state funding.[15]

5.4 Funding Follows Lobbying (Not Vice Versa)

The results in the previous section provided evidence that, on average, lobbying increases state funding for cities of all sizes across the United States. One of the key assumptions underlying this interpretation is that of parallel trends. Intuitively, this assumption states that if a lobbying city hadn't hired a lobbyist, it would have followed the same trajectory as non-lobbying cities in terms of its state transfers. Of course, we can't actually observe what lobbying cities would have gotten in the absence of that behavior. But we can inspect the trends in state funding levels for lobbying vis-à-vis non-lobbying cities before the lobbying cities picked up their contracts. Places that don't hire lobbyists might receive more or less revenue from the state, on average, compared to places that do. But if the two types of cities follow a similar pattern in their year-to-year fluctuations before the lobbying cities begin their advocacy efforts, this supports the idea that the act of lobbying is what leads to an increase in transfers.

To look for evidence of pre-treatment trends, it would be helpful to inspect the amount of state funding that lobbying and non-lobbying cities received in the years leading up to the decision to lobby. But recall that the Survey of Local Government Finances draws from a different sample of cities in each year, making it difficult to construct accurate yearly trends. I tackle this challenge in two ways. First, I examine trends for the subset of cities that appear in the Census or Survey of Local Government Finances each year (20% of the overall sample). Second, I draw from annual data on municipal finances provided by the secretaries of state of California, Washington, and Florida. These records cover all cities in these three states and can help assuage concerns that the subset of cities appearing in the Survey of Local Governments Finances are somehow systematically different from municipalities that appear less frequently.

In fact, the cities that report their finances every year in the Survey of Governments do tend to be larger than municipalities that are sampled less frequently. The average population of these cities hovers around 70,000, compared to an average population of 38,000 in the full dataset. To simplify things, I focus specifically on the set of eighty-eight cities that first disclosed lobbying activity in the 2012–2013 legislative session. Figure 5.3 plots the average yearly state transfers received between 2009 and 2014 for the places that started lobbying in 2012 or 2013 compared to places that didn't change their lobbying status during this period. Note that state transfers per capita run substantially higher for the cities in this subsample, which makes sense given how much bigger they are.

Figure 5.3 indicates that the cities that ultimately hired lobbyists typically collect more revenue per capita from the state relative to other places. But these municipalities experienced a sharp increase in their transfers after they started lobbying compared to non-lobbying cities starting in 2013. Crucially, in the period leading up to that decision, both lobbying and non-lobbying cities followed very similar trends in their year-to-year state-transfer

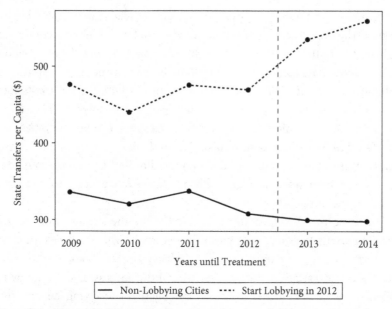

Figure 5.3 Effect of Lobbying on State Transfers: Parallel Trends. Shows the average state transfer for cities that started lobbying in the 2012–2013 legislative session compared to cities that never lobbied. Sample is drawn from cities that appear in the Survey of Local Government finances each year between 2006 and 2015.

fluctuations. If you believe that the cities that started lobbying wouldn't have received the additional funding boost without hiring a lobbyist, then we can attribute that increase to the lobbying efforts of those cities. In the chapter appendix, I more formally test for problematic pre-treatment behavior using a regression framework, and I repeat this analysis using data on the universe of municipalities in California, Washington, and Florida. In both cases, I find no evidence of concerning trends prior to the decision to lobby.

Next, I turn to the subset of twenty-seven states with reliable lobbying expenditure data to examine how the amount of money that cities spend influences their level of state funding. Recall that different states employ different disclosure laws when it comes to lobbying expenditures, with many states only requiring that clients report the name of their lobbyist and not the amount spent (see Chapter 2 for details). As a result, the majority of the analyses in this book have operationalized lobbying as a binary indicator that takes a value of 1 when a city discloses any lobbying activity in a given year.

But does the amount of money that city officials spend on lobbying matter? The average city paid just under $60,000 for its lobbying contract in a given year in the states that collect this information, with the top spender (Los Angeles) paying more than $1 million. I use the same empirical strategy outlined earlier but replace the lobbying indicator with the per capita total of reported lobbying expenditures. The results are shown graphically in Figure 5.4. For each additional dollar per capita spent on lobbying, cities generate around $8 per capita in returns. Not only does hiring a lobbyist help cities capture state revenue, but the amount allocated also seems to matter. Moreover, lobbying seems to generally be cost-effective and provide a good return on the initial investment for cities.

At this point, it's helpful to recall that despite the strong evidence that lobbying seems to "work" in terms of generating positive returns for cities on average, there are many reasons local officials might choose not to lobby. Quite a bit of variation exists in terms of how successful these lobbying efforts are, with 30 percent of lobbying cities actually receiving *less* state revenue in the years that they lobby compared to the years that they don't. City council members regularly debate whether they think the potential benefits of lobbying will outweigh the costs for their city, and many decide that the money would be better spent elsewhere. For example, Councilmember Ben Southworth of West Jordan, Utah, was one of the few city leaders who was

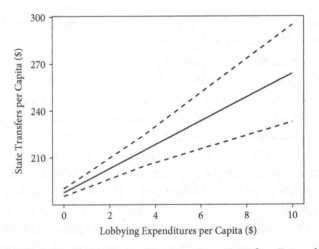

Figure 5.4 Effect of Lobbying Expenditures on State Transfers. For each additional dollar per capita spent on lobbying, cities generate around $8 per capita in returns.

skeptical about hiring Foxley & Pignanelli. He described feeling uncertain about whether the city's lobbying efforts would justify the expense. "It gives me pause when I look at that amount of money," said Southworth. "It makes me think, is this really the highest and best use of taxpayer dollars?"[16]

Other local officials describe various budgetary and political constraints that prevent them from lobbying. When Clark County, Nevada, was facing a severe budget shortfall, local officials tried to cut costs by not renewing the county's outside lobbying contract. According to one staff member, "It's difficult to justify an outside contract like that when you're laying people off."[17] Mayor Mike Houston of Springfield, Illinois, echoed this sentiment. "We have a lot of demands in terms of dollars, and we have chosen not to spend our dollars (on a lobbyist)."[18] Lobbying can also be a tough sell for the public, particularly when cities can't point to specific funding victories. "People want to know what's being accomplished, and that can be sometimes a little harder to see in a black-and-white way," explained the communications director of Anchorage, Alaska.[19]

Time horizons also affect the lobbying choices of local officials. The mayor of Taylorsville, Utah, expressed optimism about her city's decision to hire a lobbyist but cautioned, "We will be tracking the lobbying. Next year, I will report to the council exactly what funding and other benefits the city received through our lobbying efforts. Then they will have to decide whether it is worth renewing the contract."[20] Although in the long term the data suggest that lobbyists are a sound investment for cities, it makes sense that local officeholders might balk at the short-term costs if they don't see immediate results that can help their electoral prospects. Intergovernmental Affairs Director Dana Fenton of Charlotte, North Carolina, confirmed this idea. "Our council members have two-year terms, and they think in two-year intervals."[21]

5.5 Why Lobbying Benefits Rich Cities

The previous section demonstrated that cities tend to receive additional funding from their state governments after disclosing lobbying activity. But do all cities benefit equally? Existing empirical work suggests that economically powerful interests tend to dominate across a wide range of public policy outcomes (e.g., Bartels 2008; Gilens 2012; Flavin 2014). To assess whether this pattern also holds true in the context of intergovernmental lobbying,

I examine how the returns to lobbying vary across municipalities with different income levels.[22]

Figure 5.5 depicts the relationship between local income and the effect of hiring a lobbyist visually. In other words, how much more money can lobbying cities expect to earn relative to non-lobbying cities across particular median incomes? The richer the city, the higher the state transfer that accompanies the choice to lobby. Among the poorest cities in the sample (with median incomes around $36,000), lobbying actually doesn't seem to be particularly effective. But when median incomes climb above $150,000 per year, communities pick up a dramatic $50 more per capita after they start lobbying. This effect is around five times bigger than the main effect uncovered in the previous section.

Why might high-income cities experience such radically higher returns to lobbying than other types of municipalities? I consider several mechanisms that might explain this finding. One possibility is that wealthy localities might be spending more on lobbying, and perhaps cities need to spend above some threshold amount to experience positive returns. In other words, maybe poor cities just aren't investing enough money. However, the data from the subsample of states with available lobbying expenditures allow us to rule out this story. In fact, there is no correlation between city median income and the amount of money that city leaders choose to spend on lobbying.

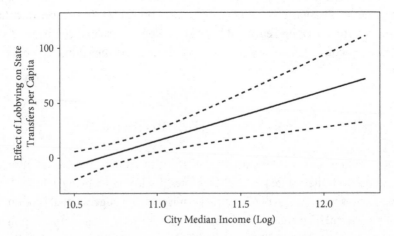

Figure 5.5 Effect of Lobbying by Median Income. As the median income of a city increases, so does the expected return on lobbying.

Another possibility is that affluent cities are more selective in their lobbying decisions and only hire lobbyists when they are confident that their efforts will be rewarded. Again, the data do not support this story. Recall in Chapter 3 that median income does not display a linear relationship with the decision to lobby. Table 5.1 shows the rates of lobbying across all cities in the sample by income category. Across years, cities in the top 25 percent of the income distribution are actually slightly more likely to lobby than cities in the bottom 25 percent. If local officials from the wealthiest cities were being more cautious in their decision to lobby, we would instead expect to see less lobbying by these cities, on average.

Next, I consider whether these high-income communities are more likely to employ effective lobbyists compared to other cities. This might be the case if prestigious lobbying firms locate more frequently in or near affluent areas. However, it turns out that a limited number of firms generally specialize in local government lobbying in each state, and these firms represent cities from across the income spectrum. In California, for example, Joe A. Gonsalves & Son and Townsend Public Affairs advocate on behalf of almost 40 percent of cities, including many wealthy suburbs as well as lower-income municipalities. Townsend Public Affairs represents Palo Alto, with a median annual household income of $120,000, as well as Huron, a small farming community in the Central Valley with a median income of just under $25,000. Cities of all economic conditions appear to have equal access to the service of professional lobbyists.

If differences in spending, frequency, and lobbying firm quality can't explain the differential returns to lobbying experienced by rich and poor cities, what can? A former mayor of Palo Alto hypothesized that the residents of

Table 5.1 City Lobbying by Income. Cities in the top 25% of the income distribution are not more likely to lobby than other cities.

Income Category	% Lobbying
Bottom 25%	12
25th–50th Percentile	18
50th–75th Percentile	19
Top 25%	16

high-income cities might pay particularly close attention to the political decisions and funding successes of their state and local officeholders. As a result, elected officials in both levels of government face strong incentives to produce results if they want to stay in office. As the mayor explained to me, "Palo Alto has folks who generally are skewed toward having higher education and incomes and expectations. People are paying close attention, and there is an attitude that 'I should get what I'm paying property tax for.' The level of property taxes and other fees that folks pay is pretty high. You get folks that themselves are vocal and engaged, and with that comes high expectations and demands on their elected officials in terms of the services that are provided and the resources that are reinvested into the neighborhood. As a result, there's basically a bottom-up demand, from my perspective, for this [state]-level engagement to happen. If there is a stream of revenue that's dedicated toward streets or schools, we must be engaging with our state elected officials to make sure we're getting our fair share. One reason that Palo Alto is so active in its advocacy efforts is because of those bottom-up expectations that you are reminded of at every council meeting."[23]

Another possibility is that wealthy cities make attractive targets for funding and grants from the perspective of budget-constrained or risk averse state officials. Affluent communities can often afford to put up matching grants to support "shovel-ready" projects with clear community benefits. A short case study of Beverly Hills illustrates this point. Over the past few decades, Beverly Hills has lobbied for programs including an Urban Water Use Efficiency Grant in 2004 and a State Homeland Security Grant for solar powered lights in 2015. The water use grant allowed the city to install low-flush toilets in municipal buildings, while the homeland security grant provided the city with emergency solar power light towers. Beverly Hills invested $44,000 in matching funds for the water grant and devised a detailed plan for maintaining the solar panels. In both cases, the projects were quickly and effectively implemented, and each had favorable environmental impacts.

To explore if other high-income cities tend to lobby for similar initiatives, I collected data on all of the bills that cities lobbied in California between 2002 and 2015.[24] I then break municipalities into income terciles and examine the text of the bill subjects lobbied by high-income communities (in the top third of the income distribution) compared to low-income places (in the bottom third). Specifically, I compare word proportions, or how frequently specific words appear relative to other words. A proportion of 1 percent indicates that a particular word comprised 1 percent of all the words mentioned in the text of the bills being lobbied. Figure 5.6 compares these word proportions for high-income versus low-income cities. The dotted line indicates that words appear at similar rates in the subjects of bills that were lobbied by both types of cities. Words falling above the dotted line were more likely to appear in the text of legislation that high-income cities targeted, while words falling below the dotted line appeared in the bills targeted by low-income cities.

The data reveal that all cities disclosed high amounts of lobbying on bills containing words like "local," "budget," "water," and "housing." But some intriguing differences also emerge in the legislative advocacy efforts of wealthy and lower-income cities. As the anecdotal evidence from Beverly Hills suggests, high-income municipalities were more likely to lobby for issues related to environmental stewardship and emissions standards. These

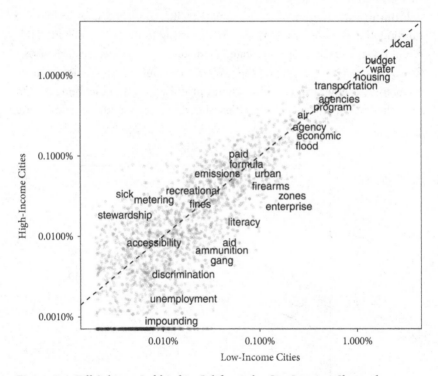

Figure 5.6 Bill Subjects Lobbied in California by City Income. Shows the most common words in the subjects of bills lobbied by cities in the top third of the income distribution (high income) or the bottom third of the income distribution (low income). Words falling above the dotted lined appear more frequently in the bills lobbied by high-income cities, and words falling below the dotted line appear more frequently in the bills lobbied by low-income cities.

communities were also very concerned about parking meters, and they targeted several bills related to paid sick leave for employees. On the other hand, the lobbyists for low-income cities tended to focus their efforts on legislation related to unemployment, state aid, literacy programs, and the establishment of enterprise zones.

Unfortunately, California doesn't require clients to disclose whether they lobbied for or against a bill. This means we can't determine whether legislation supported by high-income municipalities passed at higher rates. But what is clear from the data is that wealthier cities spread their advocacy efforts across a greater number of bills. Figure 5.7 plots the average number of bills lobbied each year by city income level. As the median income of city residents rises, local lobbyists advocate on behalf of substantially more bills each session.[25]

From the standpoint of state officials trying to decide how to allocate funding, there are several reasons why investing in cities like Beverly Hills might be an attractive option. State lawmakers may be less concerned that the money will be wasted, and the projects that high-income cities propose often address environmental issues and promise broad public benefits. On the other hand, lower-income cities generally request funding for more

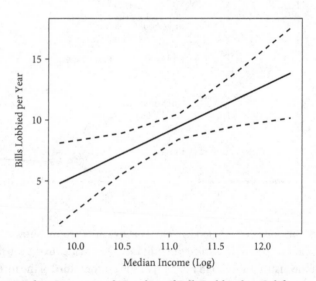

Figure 5.7 Median Income and Number of Bills Lobbied in California. As median income increases, cities report lobbying on more bills.

particularistic projects, often to support local social welfare programs. Depending on the state's goals, responding to the lobbying requests of affluent cities like Beverly Hills might make more sense from an efficiency standpoint—and would also explain why high-income cities generate substantially higher returns when they lobby.

5.6 Discussion

What do organized interests get when they lobby? This question has been surprisingly difficult for interest group scholars to answer. In their classic *Basic Interests: The Importance of Groups in Politics and in Political Science*, Baumgartner and Leech (1998) observed that empirical studies documenting what organizations get when they lobby have often produced contradictory results. They lament, "We can conclude that groups are often influential and that they are often not influential" (121). However, cities make a unique test bed to examine the returns to lobbying. State transfers provide a clear and continuous outcome measure that can be compared both across cities and within cities over time. By studying the lobbying behavior of cities, we can advance our understanding of whether and how lobbyists are able to secure benefits for the organizations they represent.

When local officials describe their decision to hire lobbyists, many liken this behavior to an investment. Securing additional revenue is one of the major goals stated in most municipal lobbying contracts, and cities will often specifically credit their lobbyists when they do manage to snag lucrative earmarks or state grants. Others describe lobbying as more like gambling and express frustration when they don't see results. City officials continuously weigh the costs and benefits of lobbying, regularly entering and exiting the state lobbying arena as they do. Anthony Gonsalves, an advocate from California, had a slightly different analogy to explain why lobbyists can be useful for cities. "My dad had a quote in the *LA Times* that we run our operation by," he told me. "'Lobbyists are like a parachute. You may not need them very often, but when you do, they had better work.'"[26] If lobbyists are like parachutes, it makes sense that communities might only choose to pay for professional lobbying services if they anticipate running into problems. Some places will always need assistance navigating state politics—like large urban centers—but others will lobby in certain legislative sessions and not others based on the issues on the agenda.

Using state transfers as an outcome measure, this chapter offered new evidence that lobbying can help cities secure state revenue. The fact that the decision to lobby increases state funding, on average, is consistent with many anecdotal accounts. But the high variance in outcomes is also consistent with the logic of gambling and helps to explain why local officials may not always be willing to spend taxpayer dollars to enter the lobbying arena. Furthermore, not all cities can expect to benefit equally from their lobbying efforts. High-income communities generate substantially higher returns compared to low-income counterparts, and this gap cannot be explained merely by differences in spending or in the quality of the lobbying firm.

One of the key assumptions in the literature on federalism is that central governments will be able to redistribute funds across regions to help offset differences in local revenue capacity, thus ensuring a basic level of service provision and horizontal economic equality across regions. And yet, empirical studies regularly find that transfer systems often exacerbate regional inequalities (e.g., Inman and Rubinfeld 1997). This pattern is exemplified by cities in the United States, where revenue inequality across municipalities has increased over the past few decades. My findings suggest that city lobbying might contribute to the puzzle of persistent inequality across local units. Affluent cities can translate their economic advantage into political power by hiring lobbyists to advance their interests, and their success can perpetuate local revenue imbalances.

One of the fundamental questions that interest group scholars grapple with is whether lobbying helps or hurts the democratic process. On the one hand, lobbying can provide critical information to elected officials and offers a way through which groups and individuals can influence government. But given differential access to resources, the population of lobbying organizations will likely not reflect the distribution of interests in society (Schattschneider 1960; Schlozman 1984).

This trade-off is starkly apparent in the case of lobbying by cities. As we saw in the first half of this book, many local leaders from a wide range of communities describe hiring lobbyists as a crucial tool for communicating their needs to the state—especially when their elected representatives are out of touch ideologically. But high-income cities appear to be particularly savvy when it comes to exerting influence through lobbying. The next chapter turns to the policy consequences of municipal lobbying and further complicates this narrative. Again, we'll see that the ability to pay for lobbyist representation introduces some degree of bias to the intergovernmental policy process. But municipal lobbying has also become more important than ever for urban, progressive cities as state legislatures attempt to curtail local control via preemption laws.

6

City vs. State

Power, Policy, and Preemption

A group of cities and their citizens in one part of the state may, through its lobbying efforts, get more state aid or tax relief; but it comes at the expense of other cities and their citizens or other public programs.

—Report on Local Government Lobbying (1990),
Minnesota Office of the Legislative Auditor

Our whole goal is to break down the issue silos and get communities to recognize the aggregate effect: that cities are constantly losing power to act on the needs and values of their residents.

—Kim Haddow,
Local Solutions Support Center

In a 2012 report commissioned by the right-leaning Show-Me Institute in Missouri, researchers analyzed dozen of lobbying contracts between local governments and their lobbying firms with the goal of understanding how these efforts impact taxpayers. They concluded that lobbying by local governments "does not lead to a just and fair distribution of public goods. It leads, instead, to an arms race of government handouts, a divisive fight for the spoils."[1] One of the key arguments in the report was that strategic lobbying by wealthy cities might "skew the distribution of power" across local communities. The report closed by calling for the Missouri Ethics Commission to collect and publicize more information about "taxpayer-funded" lobbying and for the state auditor to engage in more robust oversight of intergovernmental lobbying activities.

The previous chapter demonstrated that there may be some merit to this concern. When cities lobby, they do subsequently receive more state transfers—and high-income cities consistently receive higher returns than their less affluent counterparts. At the same time, throughout this book we've also seen evidence that lobbying can be immensely useful to local officials. It can help large, urban centers compete for equal representation in state legislatures and can assist local officials with efforts to get the attention of legislators from the opposite political party. The ability to hire lobbyists appears to be particularly useful to local leaders in states with professionalized legislatures and term limits, which often have complex policy environments. And cash-strapped localities around the country rely on lobbyists to help them secure state funding and advocate for local interests.

This chapter further complicates the simple narrative that lobbying by local governments is inherently "good" or "bad." Rather, the ability to pay for representation introduces a set of important welfare trade-offs for city leaders and residents. I begin by examining how the overall composition of lobbying cities affects resource allocation from the state's perspective. If cities are getting more state funding, where is this money coming from? And what are the net impacts of municipal lobbying on the distribution of state funds and on public policy more generally?

I find that city lobbying can indeed change the overall pattern of state funding to cities, making these transfers less progressive. But cities don't lobby for funding alone. What about the broader policy implications of this behavior? Systematically identifying the effects of lobbying on policy outcomes is challenging. Most states don't require clients to reveal which bills they are lobbying on behalf of, and the states that do have this type of disclosure law don't typically gather information on the specific position of the client. Only a handful of states—like Iowa, Nebraska, and Wisconsin—provide positions on bills lobbied, and these places have relatively low levels of municipal lobbying.

Moreover, quantitative studies of lobbying and policy passage frequently uncover null results, in part because the goal of lobbying is often to maintain the status quo or block particular bills. Hojnacki et al. (2012) followed a random sample of dozens of policy issues over time in the late 1990s and early 2000s and conducted rolling interviews with more than 300 federal lobbyists and government officials. The authors found little evidence that the lobbying efforts of interest groups mattered for policy change. They argue that these results indicate that the status quo already reflects the distribution of power based on many previous rounds of policymaking. When changes are proposed, competing interests generally mobilize on either side of an issue. These dynamics make identifying the effect of individual lobbying efforts quite challenging—especially if the goal is to conserve the existing state of affairs.

Given these challenges, I don't attempt to systematically quantify the degree of policy change that results from city lobbying. Instead, I introduce a variety of qualitative evidence and present several brief case studies that allow me to explore how city lobbying decisions shape state policies broadly. While this approach has its own weaknesses in terms of generalizability, the portrait that emerges is one of lobbyists playing a critical role for many local governments as they navigate increasingly hostile state environments. This holds particularly true for large, urban cities in red states seeking to respond to the needs and preferences of their more progressive residents. Lobbyists often play an instrumental role in helping cities to fight back against state encroachment on local control, and their efforts have featured prominently in recent preemption battles over minimum wage, gun control policies, and family leave.

So, does the ability of cities to pay for lobbyist representation help or hurt the policymaking process? The answer to this question depends on your normative framework. On the one hand, hiring lobbyists is one of the key tools available to cities as they seek to make their voices heard in other levels of government. And urban metro areas, which have become increasingly progressive over the past few decades, are often some of the most vocal proponents of lobbying. At the same time, high-income, affluent communities seem to be particularly adept at using lobbyists to move state funding in a direction that benefits them. Ultimately, if we think that places like Charlotte, North Carolina, should be able to hire lobbyists to help advance their agendas in conservative state legislatures, it means we have to accept that places like Beverly Hills and Palo Alto will be able to lobby for their interests as well—and increase their share of state funding as a result. Is this trade-off worth it? In the concluding chapter, I engage with this question in light of the evidence introduced throughout this book.

6.1 How Lobbying Shapes the Distribution of State Funding

To assess how city lobbying shapes state policy, I begin by examining the overall distribution of funding to municipalities. In the United States, states allocate most of their budgets toward K–12 education and health care, including Medicaid and various state programs for low-income residents.[2] State transfers to municipalities comprise a much smaller proportion of the overall budget. On average, around 3–5 percent of state funds are transferred directly to cities in the form of intergovernmental revenue, although in New York this figure is almost 19 percent. In practice, this amount is actually higher after accounting for state expenditures on local police programs, city public schools, transportation, and public welfare. This spending directly benefits cities and their residents but is not reported as general revenue over which municipal officials enjoy discretion. While transfers to cities make up a relatively modest portion of the total state budget, local governments depend heavily on this funding, which contribute around 20 percent of the average city's revenue.

States vary in how much flexibility they have in distributing this revenue to the local level. Some states use funding formulas that dictate how state money is allocated to municipalities, while other states employ more adaptable budgeting procedures (Perez 2008). But one of the key insights in this book is that local governments do not sit by passively waiting for state funding. Both formula-based and more discretionary transfer systems are potentially subject to influence by city lobbyists. In the former case, cities target the formulas themselves, while in the latter they lobby for individual grants and appropriations.

In thinking about how states should distribute revenue across local governments, one of the normative benchmarks often invoked in the fiscal federalism literature claims that state transfers should be designed to reduce funding disparities across localities (Musgrave 1959; Oates 1972). And yet economic inequality persists across cities, and state transfers sometimes even exacerbate this inequality. The previous chapter indicated that high-income cities capture more state revenue after lobbying than other communities. Can the lobbying behavior of cities help to explain these broader patterns of state investment?

Overall, state funding to cities appears to be largely progressive. Figure 6.1 shows the predicted value of the average transfer made to cities that fall in either the bottom third, the middle third, or the top third of the income distribution in a given state, after adjusting for population. As city income rises, transfers per capita decrease, with cities in the bottom income tercile receiving over 30 percent more revenue per capita from the state than cities

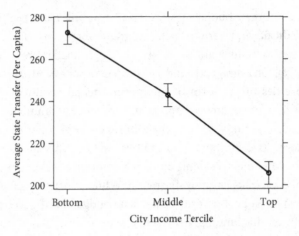

Figure 6.1 Average State Transfer by City Income Tercile. On average, states transfer more revenue per capita to low-income cities compared to high-income cities.

in the top tercile. Places with needier residents get more assistance from the state, on average.

However, substantial variation exists both within and across states in terms of how progressive their transfers are from year to year. I begin by inspecting the raw data to examine if the proportion of cities hiring lobbyists in a given year correlates with the proportion of state transfers allocated to high-income cities within each state. Figure 6.2 shows a binned scatterplot of these two values demeaned by state and year. In other words, the figure shows how within-state changes in funding vary by within-state changes in lobbying, relative to each state's own average tendencies. The raw data reveal a modest, positive correlation between overall lobbying by high-income cities—defined as cities in the top third of the income distribution for a given state—and the share of state transfers going to those cities. A 5 percentage point increase in the number of high-income cities hiring lobbyists corresponds to a small but noticeable 2.5 percentage point increase in the share of state funding allocated to those cities.

To estimate this effect more precisely, I run regressions that model the share of state transfers to high-income cities as a function of the proportion of cities lobbying plus time-varying controls such as the total state budget and the party in control of the legislature.[3] The lobbying intensity of cities continues to display a strong, positive association with the proportion of

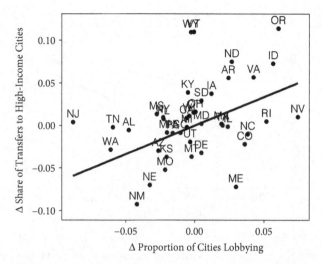

Figure 6.2 Lobbying and Share of State Transfers to High-Income Cities. Binned scatter plot shows within-state changes in the proportion of state transfers going to high-income cities against within-state changes in the proportion of cities lobbying.

state transfers being captured by high-income cities. Figure 6.3 depicts the predicted relationship between overall lobbying and state transfers graphically, and more formal estimates and additional details are shown in Table A6.1 in the chapter appendix. After at least 20 percent of municipalities in a given state start lobbying, the group of cities in the top third of the income distribution consistently net *more* than one-third of the state revenue being allocated.

These results largely complement the findings presented in Chapter 5, which indicated that at the city level, more affluent cities experience higher individual returns to lobbying than other municipalities. This section showed that, in the absence of lobbying, most state transfer systems are actually fairly progressive. Lower-income places get substantially more state assistance than high-income areas. But, as more cities lobby, states shift resources away from low-income municipalities and toward high-income cities.

In other words, the data do not paint a particularly encouraging picture of the impact of city lobbying on state funding priorities. However, it is possible that low-income and high-income cities have different goals when they lobby. After all, less affluent communities typically benefit from state funding systems designed to redistribute revenue to them. When high-income cities

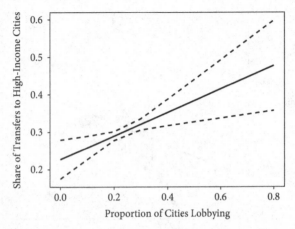

Figure 6.3 Predicted Effect of Lobbying on State Transfers to High-Income Cities. As the proportion of cities lobbying increases within a state, the share of state transfers going to high-income cities also increases.

lobby, they might do so in order to claw back revenue that would otherwise be allocated elsewhere. Other municipalities might instead focus on maintaining their existing state funding or choose to pursue different goals. What might those other goals be? I turn to this question in the next section.

6.2   Case Studies: Cities and State Preemption

Throughout this book, I've documented a variety of patterns involving the lobbying behavior of thousands of cities across the country between 2006 and 2015. In order to do this, I've had to rely primarily on both outcome and explanatory measures that lend themselves to this type of large-n statistical analysis. Are cities lobbying or not in a given year? What proportion of cities within a state are lobbying? How much money do cities get from the state when they lobby, and how does the intensity of city lobbying shape the overall distribution of state funding? But while state funding is often an important and ubiquitous goal of city lobbying, local officials also lobby for other reasons. Namely, lobbying is one of the key channels through which cities try to impact state policy.

Over the past decade, local governments have played an increasingly central role in politics and policy making in the United States. This was especially true in the years after the 2016 election of Donald Trump. With the support of their often left-leaning residents, cities emerged as the natural locus of resistance to the Trump administration. For example, shortly after his election, dozens of city mayors publicly pledged not to cooperate with forced immigrant deportation, despite the risk of losing federal funding. Even before 2016, cities were leading the way on passing policies to address climate change and increase local minimum wages, and they quickly became the new front lines for debates over immigration, sustainable growth, and social policies in the age of Trump.

At the same time, state governments have increasingly sought to limit the ability of local governments to set their own policies and regulations over the past few years. Preemption battles are playing out across the country as statehouses—often led by Republicans—attempt to harness city efforts to raise wages, regulate the sharing economy, and pass anti-discrimination measures. Amid this growing hostility from both the state and federal governments, cities are fighting back—and hiring lobbyists to help them with their efforts. In the remainder of this chapter, I present a variety of qualitative evidence and case studies that help to illustrate some of the dynamics at play as city officials navigate this new era of state-local relations.

6.3 The Rise of State Preemption

States have always had the authority to invalidate the laws of local governments within their jurisdictions. Just as federal law takes precedent over state law via the supremacy clause of the US Constitution (Article VI, Section 2), state constitutions specify which powers will be granted to local governments, and states retain the ability to change or modify those powers. Historically, states would generally use preemption sparingly in order to nullify measures that were inconsistent with state law. Doing so allowed states to create a cohesive regulatory environment and solve coordination problems among local units.

Often, such measures would take the form of policy "floors," which set minimum standards of protection that localities could build on. The same held true at the federal level. For example, the Civil Rights Act of 1964 established basic protections again discrimination, but states and cities were permitted to pass more robust protective measures and set standards above those required by federal law. Similarly, states often pass laws that create guidelines on environmental standards, and local governments can enact additional local ordinances as long as the local laws do not conflict with the state law. When states wanted to challenge local policies, they would typically do so through the courts system. This was an important channel through which states could resolve inconsistencies or disputes across jurisdictions and between state and local law.

But over the last decade, states have often focused not just on resolving inconsistencies but in hamstringing any and all efforts by cities and counties to set their own policies. In a survey of over 2,000 city officials, Barber (2016) found that 50 percent of respondents indicated that their state had successfully passed legislation that preempted local laws. Another 10 percent claimed that their state had tried to pass such a law but been unsuccessful.

Three intertwining political trends characterize this new type of preemption. First, statehouses have become more conservative since the 2010 midterm elections. This shift to the right was no accident. In 2010, conservative political strategist Karl Rove bluntly explained that if Republicans could gain control of a few key state legislative districts, they would be able to redraw the district boundaries for subsequent state and federal elections after the 2010 Census.[4] The plan worked. In 2010, Republicans held majorities in both chambers of twenty-five state legislatures and enjoyed control of both the legislature and the governorship (a "trifecta") in twenty states. By the start of 2017, these numbers had risen to thirty-two and twenty-six, respectively.

Second, while Republicans gained a foothold in statehouses across the country, urban and rural interests continued to diverge. As a recent Pew poll reported, "From feelings about President Donald Trump to views on immigration and same-sex marriage, there are wide gaps between urban and rural adults."[5] This growing geographic divide is central to American politics in the twenty-first century. Cities have become increasingly liberal (Rodden 2019) and home to creative-class workers who thrive in today's technology-driven economy (Wilkinson 2019). One of the ways in which this is reflected is in the progressive agendas being advanced by many urban metropolitan areas. As a result, state preemption today often takes the form of Republican-majority state governments overriding or preventing policies from being passed in their blue-leaning cities. While Democratic states sometimes preempt Democratic cities—for example, when Governor Cuomo of New York initially overrode New York City's plastic bag ban in 2017—many of the most salient preemption battles have played out between conservative statehouses and cities trying to enact progressive labor standards, fracking bans, environmental protections, and local anti-discrimination laws.

Finally, recent preemption efforts are closely tied to growing corporate and conservative interest group mobilization. The archetypal example is ALEC, the American Legislative Exchange Council. With its innocuous-sounding name, ALEC is a nonprofit organization that touts itself as being "the premier free-market organization that provides elected officials the resources they need to make sound policy" (deMarrais et al. 2019). Founded in the 1970s, ALEC has grown into one of the most influential interest groups in the United States. Essentially, the group connects corporate clients with state legislators in order to drum up support for business-friendly policies.[6] In fact, ALEC often writes model legislation, including preemption bills, that can be imitated and quickly adopted from state to state. A copy of a bill designed to preempt local minimum wage increases is posted on the ALEC website.[7] By some estimates, ALEC has produced hundreds of model policies that have made their way into state codes.[8]

6.4 How Cities Are Responding

City officials have actively fought back against state preemption. One of the tools at their disposal is the court system. In some states, cities have tried to make the case that state preemption laws are unconstitutional because they overstep home rule provisions or because they single out particular localities. This has been the preferred strategy of cities in Florida, which have pursued legal means to overturn state laws banning them from passing local gun control measures. After the 2018 mass shooting at Marjory Stoneman Douglas High School in Parkland, a group of ten cities including Weston, Coral Gables, Cutler Bay, Lauderhill, Miami Beach, Miami Gardens, Miramar, Pinecrest, Pompano Beach, and South Miami banded together to sue the state's governor. The lawsuit targeted a 2011 law that prohibits local governments from enacting their own gun regulations. Raul Aguila, the city attorney for Miami Beach, explained, "Year after year, the Legislature gets bolder and more outrageous in using [preemption] to prohibit local governments from passing progressive legislation."[9]

More cities quickly joined the suit, and the lower courts ultimately ruled in their favor. While the case works its way through the appeals process, municipal officials remain hopeful that the state will side with them and allow cities to pass local gun control measures, such as regulating gun sales within city-boundaries or declaring certain public spaces as gun-free zones. According to Jamie Cole, a lawyer with one of the private firms representing the cities, "Municipalities and elected officials from across the state, in urban, suburban and rural communities, have all joined the fight to protect the home rule authority of local governments, and to reflect the passion of their residents."[10]

In other regions of the country, cities have brought similar suits that seek to legally invalidate state laws. Cleveland successfully won a lawsuit against the State of Ohio over a preemption law designed to restrict local hiring. However, in Alabama a federal appeals court ruled that workers in Birmingham didn't have standing to advance a lawsuit challenging the state law that preempted Birmingham's attempted minimum wage increase. While city attorneys and private law firms are the primary figures orchestrating these legal challenges, by far more activity is occurring in the legislative arena as city officials attempt to either prevent these laws from passing in the first place or usher in legislation that would overturn previous preemption laws. As Schragger (2017) observed in a recent law review piece, "Very little preemptive legislation is ultimately susceptible to legal challenge. Instead, city resistance normally takes place within the legislative arena, in fights over legislation and repeal" (1126). And professional lobbyists representing both individual cities and municipal leagues are leading the charge on this front.

In Florida, for example, several cities were among the most vocal supporters of the gun control package that the state legislature passed in 2018.[11] This legislation raised the minimum age to purchase firearms, imposed a waiting period on gun purchases, and provided funding for mental health counselors and school police officers, among other measures. Even if city legal efforts to overturn local gun control preemption laws prove unsuccessful, their ability to shape other legislation related to public safety remains an important political weapon. Florida lobbyist Ron Book told me he is proud to be part of that fight. "Local governments in Florida right now—and for the last six years—have been under attack," Book said. "The state wants to preempt their authority to do this, their authority to do that. I'm constantly fighting those battles on behalf of my local governments. I represent thirty-plus cities and counties, a school district, and several special districts, and I fight like hell to protect them and to make certain that their voices are heard when appropriate."[12]

In other states, cities have enjoyed more success lobbying to overturn preemptive state laws. Take Colorado, which in 1999 passed legislation prohibiting cities and counties from adopting their own minimum wage ordinances. The law faced little push back initially, as the state boasted fairly progressive prevailing wages. In 2006, voters approved Initiative 42, which raised the state's minimum wage to $6.85 an hour with adjustments for inflation. Another amendment in 2016 further increased the minimum wage to $12 per hour over a multi-year phase-in period. But as cities across the country began experimenting with their own higher minimum wages, local leaders in Colorado eventually organized to mount an aggressive campaign to support HB1210, a bill that would repeal existing law and expressively grant cities and counties the ability to adopt and enforce their own minimum wages.

Lobbyists for the Colorado Municipal League as well as for individual municipalities proved crucial in garnering support for the measure. The local government lobby provided extensive research from other states demonstrating that cities and counties could raise their minimum wages without harming the competitiveness of either the local economy or surrounding areas. Proponents of the measure also emphasized the significant benefits that low-wage workers and families experience when wages increase, including better education and health outcomes.[13] Of all the lobbying activity performed on behalf of HB 1210, 10 percent of reported meetings took place between individual city lobbyists and lawmakers.[14] And despite facing powerful opposition from the Colorado Chamber of Commerce and Farmer's Bureau, the bill ultimately passed, marking the first time a state legislature has repealed an existing minimum wage preemption law. Similar pieces of legislation have since been introduced in eleven other states, including Texas, Indiana, and New York.

A similar story played out in Maryland, where individual cities and the League of Maryland Municipalities played an instrumental role in helping to pass a new minimum wage law. In 2019, Maryland became the sixth state to enact a $15 minimum wage. Although Republican governor Larry Hogan initially vetoed the legislation, Democrats in the state legislature were able to achieve the two-thirds vote necessary to override the veto. The real victory for local governments, however, was the fact that the new law explicitly allowed cities and counties to set their own, higher minimum wages, which hadn't previously been permitted.

Supporting the Maryland minimum wage bill constituted a major goal of the Maryland Municipal League in that legislative session, and individual cities also hired lobbyists to help voice their support. The number of municipalities filing lobbyist disclosure forms in Maryland increased from fifteen in the 2015 legislative session to twenty-five in the legislative session leading up to the passage of the bill, suggesting that local officials mobilized in response to the issue. The City of Rockville even issued an RFP in 2018 that requested legislative advocacy services and stressed that fighting against pre-emption and maintaining local control would be key objectives for the city's lobbyist.[15]

Cities across the country have also successfully repealed or amended non-minimum wage related preemption bills. For example, the League of Connecticut Municipalities and individual cities actively testified before the Public Health Committee to encourage passage of a 2017 bill that would amend language preempting municipal ordinances on smoking regulations.[16] And a report on preemption from the New America Foundation states that many of the recent successes that local officials have experienced occur at the committee stage and thus don't make headlines. According to the re-port, "In Texas and Florida in the 2019 legislative session, local democ-racy advocates helped kill multiple preemption bills in committee—and in behind-the-scenes negotiations between House Democratic and Republican leadership—which would have likely passed had they gone to a floor vote."[17]

It bears repeating: one of the reasons why it's so difficult to identify the effects of city lobbying is because so much of this activity happens under the radar. As Alaska lobbyist Myer Hutchinson observed, "It's not always about the bills that are passed but the bills that are stopped, or the bills that are changed."[18] For each of the policies I have described, dozens of other groups mobilized both in favor of and against the positions taken by lobbying cities. One of the key benefits that professional lobbyists offer their local govern-ment clients is the ability to mobilize quickly when a window of opportunity arises, as was the case in Florida after the Stoneman Douglas High School massacre. And even when cities don't achieve visible victories, their lobbying efforts may well help to preserve the status quo against new preemption measures that are often backed by groups like the NRA or ALEC.

6.5 What Do City Lobbying Efforts against Preemption Look Like?

The specific lobbying tactics that local lobbyists use to wage these battles against preemption are largely similar to those discussed in Chapter 2. The emphasis is typically on conducting research to convince lawmakers why legislation would be either good or bad for cities and constituents within the state. Lobbyists help local governments craft position papers and facilitate meetings between state and local officials.[19] The National League of Cities advises cities to pick their preemption battles carefully and suggests using the language of "local democracy" whenever possible. Kim Winn, the executive director of the Virginia Municipal League, says the lobbyists for her organization focus their energy on providing information to legislators, who frequently do not understand how bills would affect cities they do not represent.[20]

Oftentimes, the lobbying efforts of cities hold weight with state lawmakers precisely because state lawmakers value information about district priorities. California advocate Anthony Gonsalves explained to me, "It's all about their base. [State legislators] want to protect themselves and their district. Sometimes, they may be getting misinformation from the person carrying the legislation or from outside interest groups. Our job is to let them know how particular legislation impacts the cities in their district. I'd say 99 percent of the time, when they get the proper information about how a bill impacts their district, they're going to vote for their district."[21]

One of the trends in the area of city lobbying is that new coalitions of legal scholars, lobbyists, and local officials have formed in order to share information and tactics with each other. For example, the Local Solutions Support Center (LSSC) is a national hub that was founded in 2017 to coordinate city efforts to counter state preemption. The stated goals of the center are to raise awareness about preemption, block preemptive legislation, and increase local government control over public policies. It does so by working across four integrated areas: legal strategy, education and outreach, communications and research, and grassroots organizing. According to the LSSC website, they accomplish these goals by "educating and connecting city attorneys, state and local elected officials, and advocates facing preemption threats, providing direct legal and strategic assistance, developing research and messaging to re-frame the debate around preemption, building cross-issue coalitions at the local, state, and national levels, and providing advocates and policymakers with strategies and tools to counter preemption and advance equity-promoting policies."[22]

One successful strategy the center has employed includes conducting polls that demonstrate public support for local control. In Florida, one such poll asked whether respondents agree that local officials "should generally be able to pass local laws to protect public health, the environment, and quality jobs when a community believes that statewide laws aren't enough." The research showed that 81 percent of respondents agreed, while only 13 percent disagreed. Findings like these can be a powerful tool for cities trying to convince state legislators that constituents are wary of state preemptive measures. Kim Haddow, director of LSSC, reports that poll results like these consistently indicate that "Floridians rightly believe that local elected officials are closer to the people in their communities and understand their values and needs better than lawmakers in Tallahassee, and that's why they trust local governments to make local decisions."[23]

The Legal Effort to Address Preemption (LEAP) provides another example of a recent coalition formed to assist cities. This group consists of a network of legal scholars, lobbyists, and advocates, and—similar to LSSC—their mission is to "devise strategies and create resources to protect the authority and power of cities to enact inclusive, innovative, evidence-based, and equitable laws."[24] To help support cities of all sizes in the fight against preemption, LEAP employs several tactics. These include facilitating peer networking for city officials that allows them to share information about preemption challenges and successes; developing a network of lobbyists and attorneys that specialize in municipal affairs and can assist city efforts; conducting research and educating the legal, elected, and advocacy communities about preemption issues; and providing briefings and reports to local elected officials about their options for countering state interference.[25] Advocates of this approach note that many small and mid-sized cities have limited capacity and resources and lack full-time intergovernmental relations staff or city attorneys. The result is growing demand for information and assistance from outside sources and professional lobbyists.

It's unclear how long this current chapter in municipal-state relations will last. Ironically, the preemption battles playing out across the country often flip the traditional script of liberal and conservative views on decentralization. The GOP has long positioned itself as the party of local government and has criticized Democrats for trying to dictate the policy agenda from Washington, DC. But after years of seeing progressive local reforms overturned by preemption efforts led by red statehouses, Democrats are now championing decentralization and local control. According to political scientist Riverstone-Newell (2017), "If the pattern that has developed over the past several years holds, local governments can expect to lose even more power, to have their decisions undone, to face legal challenges, and to face personal and jurisdictional penalties for actions the state determines to be 'overreach.'" As long as this is true, powerful incentives will remain for local governments to rely on lobbyists to help them navigate these challenges.

6.6 Discussion

This chapter presented competing evidence on the ways in which city lobbying influences the overall state-level policy environment. On one hand, one of the major goals that local officials articulate when choosing to hire lobbyists is to secure funding. When I examine how lobbying correlates with the aggregate distribution of state funding across municipalities, the data suggest that local lobbying efforts contribute to resources being shifted away from less affluent communities and toward higher-income places. While state transfer systems are largely progressive, on average, and allocate more revenue per capita to lower-income municipalities, they become more regressive as the number of cities hiring lobbyists increases. Municipal lobbying doesn't just yield higher returns for individual cities: it shifts the entire distribution of state funding toward higher-income areas.

But, at the same time, one of the other key objectives of lobbying is to shape public policy and to amplify city voices and interests at the state level. On this front, we see many local officials from cities of all types describing their lobbyists as "essential"[26] and "a great tool to get attention for a city."[27] The ability for local officials to hire lobbyists has become particularly important over the last decade. State legislatures have waged a series of preemption battles against their local governments, preventing cities from passing their own ordinances to increase minimum wages, regulate gun sales, and set environmental standards. These preemption efforts emerged in the wake of cities steadily asserting themselves as the face of the resistance to the former Trump administration and amid growing urban-rural polarization. And the types of cities that are most likely to engage in this kind of policy-focused lobbying tend to be urban metropolitan centers that are increasingly progressive—especially those in conservative-leaning states like Alabama, Florida, and Arizona.

So what are the net welfare consequences? Is it worth allowing affluent municipalities to hire lobbyists to compete for additional grants and state transfers if it means that cities both large and small can lobby to fend off state preemption efforts? There are no simple answers. This chapter lays bare the trade-off that has appeared throughout the book. Lobbying can be enormously helpful to local officials from cities of all types. Both in-house and hired lobbyists can help cities advance their policy agenda when they have ideological disagreements with either their state delegation or the state government as a whole. This appears to be particularly true for the largest, most diverse, most progressive cities. At the same time, lobbying can also exacerbate inequality by giving economically powerful communities another channel through which to exercise influence. What are we to make of these competing facts? In the Conclusion, I discuss the normative implications of these findings as well as prospects for reform.

7

Conclusion

Why Cities Lobby and Why It Matters

Government can't even talk to itself without hiring private lobbyists to help grease the wheels.

—Bill Mahoney,
New York Public Interest Research Group

I think people think of lobbyists as a really negative, nefarious figure, and really it's about having better coordination between governments because we do all share constituents and are trying to find more efficient outcomes.

—Elizabeth Edwards,
City of Portland, Office of Government Relations

When asked why he decided to hire a lobbyist for his city, Mayor Mike Spano of Yonkers, New York, explained: "Lobbyists are an essential part of moving the process. I can't live up [in Albany]. I can't be up here for every detail."[1] As this book has demonstrated, many other local officials employ similar logic. Across the country, thousands of local governments spend hundreds of millions of dollars to lobby other levels of government every year. Collectively, they make up one of the largest and most understudied state-level interest groups in the United States.

This book focused on the lobbying behavior of municipalities—the most common general purpose government at the local level. The chapters in this volume provided new quantitative, qualitative, and historical evidence to construct the most detailed portrait to date about what happens when cities lobby. In particular, new longitudinal data on municipal lobbying in all fifty states allowed me to uncover several important empirical patterns about the types of cities that lobby, what they get as a result, and how this behavior shapes the distribution of state spending and policy priorities.

One of the main theoretical insights developed in this book is that local governments differ from most other interest groups as a result of their position within the federal system. To understand when and why cities lobby, we need to understand their political geography. In general, city leaders are highly sensitive to the policy and funding decisions made by state-level actors. State laws and regulations shape and constrain the policy options available to local officials, and cities often rely heavily on the state for transfers and revenue. While city officials are attuned to the decisions of many state actors across the various branches of government, their relationship with their elected delegation in the legislature is particularly important. The data reveal that the political dynamics of a city's state legislative district matter a great deal for local lobbying decisions and suggest that lobbyists can help bridge the representational gaps that sometimes emerge in multilevel government.

This is particularly true in states with both professionalized legislatures and term limits. City leaders in these states often describe the complexity of intergovernmental affairs and insist that hiring lobbyists is the only way for them to navigate the shifting and intricate policy environment. According to one lobbyist in California, "The range of issues is so vast and complex that cities, counties and other government entities need a full-time presence to watch what's happening, or they could wind up hit with an unfunded mandate or a badly needed road project zeroed out."[2] Given the complicated informational environment, legislators in these states are also especially likely to value input from lobbyists representing city officials in their district, who have direct knowledge of local challenges and priorities.

But municipal lobbying also has its downsides. Although all local governments maintain the ability to hire lobbyists, wealthy communities have become particularly adept at strategically using lobbyists to secure additional grant money and shift state funding in a direction that favors them. Strikingly, cities in the top of the income distribution enjoy an increase in state transfers per capita that is thirty times that of cities in the bottom third—and most of these benefits accrue to the top wealthiest 10 percent of cities. As a result, lobbying appears to provide another channel through which affluent areas can translate their economic advantage into political clout.

We are left with a simple question. Are we willing to accept that certain communities might benefit disproportionately from lobbying if it means granting a stronger voice to cities of all types—including the progressive, urban metro areas that served as the face of the resistance to the former Trump administration? The ability to hire lobbyists is a powerful tool that, in the aggregate, both empowers local governments and also introduces many of the classic equity concerns more typically associated with interest group behavior. How should we evaluate the net consequences of this behavior for society in light of the evidence provided in this book?

Arguments that conclude that the price of municipal lobbying outweighs the benefits typically fall into three categories. The first consists of conservative critiques that focus on the costs to taxpayers and, often implicitly, seek to limit progressive local policy trends. The second category offers egalitarian arguments that emphasize the ways in which lobbying might exacerbate local inequality. And the third set of arguments highlights broader concerns about institutional design and interest representation in the United States. How did we end up with a system where lobbyists play such a prominent role in state and local politics? I discuss the merits and relevant considerations of each of these arguments in turn.

7.1 Conservative Critiques of Municipal Lobbying

Conservatives who object to the idea of "taxpayer-funded lobbying" offer some of the most scathing criticisms of the practice of local governments hiring lobbyists. Phil Kerpen summarized this position in a *National Review* piece, writing, "While ordinary Americans are busy working, their hard-earned tax dollars are being used to pay lobbyists who are fighting for higher taxes and bigger government."[3] Proponents of this view take issue with the fact that this behavior is paid for with tax revenue, often with the goal of growing the overall size of the state budget. Many conservative state legislators claim to share similar concerns, and lawmakers have introduced measures to limit local government lobbying in states ranging from Texas and Florida to Oklahoma and Arizona. According to Minnesota Rep. Steve Drazkowski, who expresses frustration with the practice, "Our municipalities are spending way, way, way too much of the property taxpayer money simply to go to St. Paul to try to chase more taxpayer money with it. And that's the problem I think that I and a number of other legislators have."[4]

However, it's not clear that banning intergovernmental lobbying would actually save taxpayer money. If local officials were unable to hire professional lobbyists, that wouldn't prevent them from employing intergovernmental relations officials on their staff. And for many cities, it would likely cost more to pay the full-time salaries and benefits of additional city employees relative to the costs of a quarterly or yearly contract with a lobbying firm. Outside lobbyists also offer several advantages to cities that regular staff members can't, including their extensive networks with state officials and the ability for cities to quickly and flexibly mobilize in certain periods but not others. It's also worth noting that the public nature of local government lobbying might also be thought of in positive terms. Precisely because cities represent democratically elected bodies and are funded by taxpayers, the actions of city officials are subject to greater public scrutiny and accountability than many other interest groups. If voters are unhappy with the choices of their local officeholders—including the decision to lobby—they can express this dissatisfaction at the ballot box.

While opponents of local government lobbying often claim that elected officials themselves should be the ones to communicate local priorities to higher levels of government, issues mire this approach as well. The city manager of Plant City, Florida, justified his choice to hire a lobbyist by noting, "We've got full-time jobs back here, managing the city."[5] The time and effort that city officials spend on "lobbying" is time and effort not spent on other activities. As the city manager of Burbank, California, pointed out, "The public perception of our council members making trips to Sacramento and Washington has also been called into question. . . . I think any way you slice it, influencing legislation and making sure that your residents receive what you feel is in their best interest takes time and money."[6]

While conservatives typically cloak their concerns about intergovernmental lobbying in language that emphasizes taxpayers and the size of government, there also appears to be a political angle to these critiques. Many of the most active city lobbyists represent large, progressive, urban areas—especially in predominantly Republican states in the south. While conservative legislators may be genuinely concerned about the fiscal implications of municipal lobbying, it is also true that many of the municipalities that lobby are blue-leaning relative to the rest of the state. When cities pass progressive local ordinances, Republicans often frame their opposition in terms of wanting to avoid a regulatory patchwork of policies that might make the state less competitive to businesses (Riverstone-Newell 2017). But city officials are more likely to say that recent preemption measures or attempts to limit intergovernmental lobbying are simply ill-disguised endeavors to hamstring areas that typically support the other political party.[7]

Your perspective on this debate likely depends on your ideological leanings. But it's important to remember that, at different points in time, Republicans and Democrats alike have championed the idea of federalism and local control. Traditionally, Republicans have extolled the virtues of small government that operates closer to the people. But under Republican administrations, Democrats have been eager to allow states and cities to experiment with local autonomy—particularly when those experiments involve higher minimum wages, paid family leave, and environmental protections. As Rodden (2019) writes, "Republicans will surely rediscover their traditional affection for federalism and local control when the Democrats return to power" (14). In other words, there is nothing inherently conservative or liberal about granting power to local governments to advocate for their interests. While there are many legitimate concerns that people might raise about the rise of local government lobbying, limiting this activity simply based on the partisan dynamics of the moment does not seem like a particularly effective strategy.

7.2 Does Municipal Lobbying Exacerbate Inequality?

Another set of arguments against local government lobbying include egalitarian critiques. According to this perspective, we might want to think long and hard about who benefits from the ability to hire lobbyists before allowing this behavior to flourish unchecked. This is the classic concern voiced by interest group scholars going back to Schattschneider (1960), who cautioned that the "business or upper-class bias of the pressure system shows up everywhere" (30). Similarly, given variation in access to resources, the distribution of lobbying cities might not reflect the interests of the country as a whole.

The data introduced in this book indicate that this concern is valid. While city size is the most important predictor of lobbying activity, cities with robust tax bases and higher median home values also lobby frequently, all else equal. When they do, they generate substantially higher returns in terms of state funding. However, in the absence of lobbying, wealthy places would still likely enjoy a variety of built-in advantages. Affluent communities generally have more politically active residents (Verba, Schlozman, and Brady 1995), and it might be easier for them to afford to employ in-house intergovernmental relations staff. It's unclear whether the effects of paid lobbying simply mimic existing patterns of inequality or if this behavior actually exacerbates them.

A sensible path forward to address this issue might include both more research and greater reporting transparency by state governments. States might opt to collect and publicize information about the lobbying behavior of their local units in a more systematic way in order to identify potential sources of bias. For example, are earmarks, grants, or appropriations disproportionately channeled to cities that pay for lobbyist representation? It may be that, as scholars and public officials continue to gather information and study this topic, the possible equity concerns become more stark. But while we should certainly be sensitive to the ways in which intergovernmental lobbying might perpetuate inequality, it's also useful to think about the reasons why cities lobby so much in the first place.

7.3 Intergovernmental Lobbying and Democratic Representation

A final set of arguments specifically addresses these root incentives of city lobbying. Ostensibly, the US federal system provides "normal" channels of representation to cities via their state and federal elected officials (Loftis and Kettler 2015). What does it say about access to power if local officials have to pay lobbyists to communicate with their counterparts in other levels of government? Many cities—and particularly large metropolitan cores—face representational disadvantages by virtue of their political geography. Partisan gerrymandering and the geographic clustering of urban voters ensures that rural interests are often overrepresented in both state legislatures and congressional districts. And municipalities of all sizes may face variation in the quality of their vertical representation from time to time. If the goal is to reduce the influence of private lobbyists in intergovernmental policymaking, perhaps we should focus on addressing the design of our representational institutions that make lobbying such an attractive (and often necessary) option in the first place.

Of course, the structural difficulties facing American cities are deeply entrenched. Our winner-take-all electoral system, the way in which legislative districts are drawn and redrawn, and the anti-majoritarian features of the US government collectively conspire to give voice and power to less populous areas at the expense of the places where the majority of residents live. These issues are challenging and sticky, and dramatic structural shifts would likely be required in order to address them. The political willpower to do so may or may not materialize anytime soon. In the meantime, hiring lobbyists seems like an inevitable and relatively efficient way for local officials to assert their voices in the intergovernmental policymaking process.

Additionally, it's important to recognize that local governments are not lobbying in a vacuum. Interest group activity in the states has increased dramatically, in all sectors, especially since the 1980s. If we attempt to limit cities from lobbying while permitting corporate and other special interests to lobby unchecked, we needlessly exclude an important set of voices from the debate. Unless elected officials are willing to enact more general, systematic reforms that fundamentally change the role that professional lobbyists play in the way our government operates, it makes little sense to begin by targeting local governments.

7.4 The View from Above and Below

In the final part of this chapter, I discuss several policy proposals that have been put forward with the goal of changing or regulating the way in which city officials use lobbyists to represent local interests. In order to assess these proposals, it seems useful to first identify the major groups that stand to gain or lose from this behavior. What do citizens, local officials, and state actors say about their preferences and concerns regarding the lobbying behavior of cities?

In general, the public doesn't seem to know much about the lobbying activities of their local governments. While we lack systematic data to this effect, elected politicians often mention that constituents are "shocked" or "surprised" when they learn that local governments hire lobbyists.[8] Some opponents of intergovernmental lobbying claim that taxpayers shouldn't be forced to support lobbying efforts they may or may not support. But this argument doesn't have much bite. Governments use tax dollars for all sorts of activities that residents may or may not like, know about, or consent to. City residents benefit when their communities are flourishing. It is likely that public attitudes toward local government lobbying are heavily tied to how successful their cities are when they lobby. Classic work in urban political economy also emphasizes that residents can relocate to other places if they are unhappy with the bundle of public goods and services provided in their neighborhoods (e.g., Tiebout 1956; Peterson 1981). From this perspective, local officials should strive to match their local policies to public preferences—and residents also have the option of moving. If lobbying can help local officeholders meet community needs, then the net welfare effect for city residents is probably positive.

Local officials themselves are often among the most vocal defenders of their right to hire lobbyists. They describe the complexities of state government and argue that it would be "unrealistic" for them to keep up with thousands of bills each legislative session.[9] One mayor described the ability to lobby as crucial for "protecting our ability to make decisions at the local level rather than have state government dictate what we do."[10] Local officials call their lobbyists "a great tool"[11] who open "doors of communication" and are "worth their weight in gold."[12]

Some local leaders lament that it needs to be this way. A county official in Michigan explained, "I didn't create the system . . . I just have to live by those rules. We're competing with every other group for funding."[13] The mayor of Flagstaff, Arizona, agreed: "If we don't take an active part in getting those earmarks, they're going to go somewhere else. Until the game changes we're going to play by these current rules."[14] But, for now, the name of the game is lobbying. Most city leaders acknowledge that, in the absence of broader reform, lobbyists play an important role in helping them to achieve their goals.

State legislators are the group who typically express the most skepticism about city lobbying. They often seem to equate lobbying by local officials with a personal affront on their effectiveness as representatives. At the federal level, Senator Byrd of West Virginia once famously quipped, "Why do you waste your money on a lobbyist when I'm being paid to be your senator?" State lawmakers express similar sentiments, calling it "insulting" or "unnecessary" when local governments in their district hire lobbyists.[15] "The mayor has my cellphone number," said the speaker of the Tennessee House of Representatives. "He can call me anytime."[16]

And yet, for all their political bluster, local lobbying can also be helpful to state legislators. City lobbyists provide state lawmakers with useful information about local conditions and constituent preferences. One of the primary jobs of state representatives is to meet regularly with the mayors and city council members in their district (Jewell 1982), and lobbyists provide another channel through which communication can happen. On their websites, it's common for state elected officials to list the cities in the district. State legislators clearly care about representing the interests of the local governments in their jurisdiction. While many publicly profess to prefer direct communication with local leaders, some acknowledge that lobbyists can play an important role in facilitating conversations. "I get valuable information from those who lobby on behalf of local communities," admitted Rep. Clark Johnson of Minnesota.[17] And New York State Assembly Member Shelly Mayer told me, "We see the lobbyists as partners for getting funding for the city and school district."[18]

7.5 Prospects for Reform

A 2012 policy brief issued by the Missouri Show-Me Institute articulated three main reforms that states might consider if they are concerned about the lobbying activity of their local units. The first encourages states to ensure that their lobby disclosure laws and reporting systems are designed to collect and display a greater range of information about the lobbying efforts of local governments. The second proposes that state auditors and ethics commissions perform regular audits on the lobbying behavior of their public entities to gather additional data on the goals and consequences of this activity. And the third discusses banning or limiting the behavior outright—which, as I discussed in Chapter 4, several states have recently attempted to do.

When it comes to regulating interest group activity, political scientists are generally the most bullish on the first of these options. As Thomas and Hrebenar (2004) describe in their groundbreaking study on state interest group activity, "The greatest value of lobby laws and other lobby regulations is in providing information on who is lobbying whom. Disclosure increases the potential for public and, particularly, press scrutiny of lobbying. Increased public information has probably been the element of lobby regulation that has had the most significant effect on state politics and government" (139). There seems to be little reason for states not to adopt lobby disclosure reporting standards that are strict, transparent, and publicly accessible.

Many states have also begun experimenting with the second proposal. Arizona and Washington created separate pages on their ethics websites where they break down lobbying disclosures by public versus private entities, making it easy for journalists, lawmakers, and the public to identify which local governments are spending money to hire lobbyists. The Office of the State Auditor of Minnesota releases a regular report on the use of local government lobbying services in the state. The report highlights trends in local lobbying behavior over time, discusses the state agencies and legislators toward which the advocacy efforts are aimed, and provides detailed information about expenditure patterns.[19] Efforts like this might be particularly attractive to help reveal potential equity concerns that accompany lobbying by local governments. In which states are high-income communities that employ lobbyists getting a disproportionate share of state grants? Which types of cities are left out of this process? More rigorous state oversight of intergovernmental advocacy activities can help shed light on these questions.

The last reform proposal, outright bans or limitations on intergovernmental lobbying, has received the most attention in the media in recent years. However, it is unlikely that these efforts will succeed any time soon. For decades, courts across the country have been unwavering in upholding the right of local units to lobby (Berman 2003). Attempts by legislators to introduce bills to curb "taxpayer-funded lobbying" appear to be mostly for political show. Even when minor victories are achieved—for example, when a court ruled that the Texas Association of Counties couldn't use membership dues to hire lobbyists—a variety of straightforward workarounds generally exist. In the Texas Association of Counties case, the court indicated that the Association merely needed to segregate its funds on its financial statements in order to carry on with its lobbying efforts.

States may well continue to explore bans on local government lobbying—especially if state-local relations continue to be characterized by preemption battles and increasing urban-rural polarization. But as I discussed earlier, in the absence of more widespread structural reform to the broader lobbying industry, it seems difficult to argue that banning cities from lobbying would alone lead to better policy outcomes.

What seems clear is that intergovernmental relations in the twenty-first century are increasingly complex. The right to lobby is currently protected and deeply interwoven in the fabric of our democracy. Given the immense challenges facing cities, including increasing hostility from state legislatures, we are in a period when municipalities of all types and sizes need as many tools in their arsenal as possible when it comes to defending local interests and shaping state policy. The incentives for local governments to lobby are built into the representational structure of our federal system. As a result, it seems likely that lobbyists will continue to play a critical role for local officials seeking to advocate for their interests in state politics for years to come.

Appendices

Chapter 2 Appendix

Table A2.1 shows the sources and structure of the state-level lobbying data used throughout this book. Every state requires the names of clients that engage in lobbying to be disclosed, and forty-two states also make it possible to link clients with the names of the lobbyists representing them. However, only nine states also include the name of the lobbying firm representing them, which makes it difficult to know whether cities are employing internal or external lobbyists. Only the largest cities tend to staff intergovernmental affairs officers in-house. This type of lobbying tends to be fairly consistent from year to year, and the key source of the variation in the data comes from cities starting and stopping their contracts with external lobbyists over the course of the decade. For many analyses in the book, the unit of observation is the client-year, and the key independent variable is an indicator that takes a value of 1 if clients had any reported lobbying in a particular year.

It's worth reiterating that states vary somewhat in their disclosure laws. The National Conference of State Legislatures provides several helpful resources that clarify how states define "lobbying" and "lobbyist" and summarize the main differences in reporting requirements across states.[1] For example, some states only require disclosure if lobbyists receive above a certain amount of compensation (often $2,000 or $5,000) or spend a certain amount of time lobbying (often five hours or more per month). Any measurement error introduced by the exclusion of nominal lobbying efforts below these thresholds should only serve to attenuate the results. Moreover, in most analyses I include state by year fixed effects, which allows me to flexibly control for state-level differences in disclosure records.

Table A2.2 provides details about the number of years of lobbying data available for each state, the number of cities with a population above 5,000, and summary statistics on lobbying expenditures for the states with reliable spending data. Some states regularly end up falling out of the analyses simply due to the small number of cities with populations above this threshold. For example, the only incorporated city in Hawaii is Honolulu.

Figure A2.1 shows an excerpt from a Palo Alto City Council Staff Report that describes the city's lobbying goals. Cities are generally quite transparent about what they hope to achieve via lobbying and often make the content of their RFPs or even the lobbying contracts themselves available on their city council websites.

2.1 State Lobbying Disclosure Data Summary.

e	Website	Data Structure	Data Available
Alabama	http://ethics.alabama.gov/LobbyistList.aspx	Client, lobbyist	Client names only
Alaska	http://doa.alaska.gov/apoc/SearchReports/reports.html#lobbying	Client, lobbyist	All expenditures
Arizona	http://www.azsos.gov/elections/lobbyists/historical-expenditure-summaries	Client	All expenditures
Arkansas	http://www.sos.arkansas.gov/lobbyist_search/index.php/search/advanced/new	Client, lobbyist, firm	Partial expenditures
California	http://cal-access.sos.ca.gov/lobbying/	Client, lobbyist, firm	All expenditures
Colorado	https://www.sos.state.co.us/lobby/Home.do	Client, lobbyist	Client names only
Connecticut	https://www.oseapps.ct.gov/NewLobbyist/security/loginhome.aspx	Client, lobbyist, firm	All expenditures
Delaware	https://egov.delaware.gov/lobs/Explore/ExploreLobbyists	Client, lobbyist	Client names only
Florida	https://floridalobbyist.gov/	Client, lobbyist, firm	All expenditures
Georgia	http://media.ethics.ga.gov/search/Lobbyist/Lobbyist_Menu.aspx	Client, lobbyist	Partial expenditures
Hawaii	http://ethics.hawaii.gov/orgexp/	Client	Client names only
Idaho	http://www.sos.idaho.gov/elect/lobbyist/disclosures.html	Client, lobbyist	Partial expenditures
Illinois	http://www.ilsos.gov/lobbyistsearch/	Client, lobbyist, firm	Partial expenditures
Indiana	http://www.in.gov/ilrc/2335.htm	Client, lobbyist	All expenditures
Iowa	https://www.legis.iowa.gov/lobbyist/reports	Client, lobbyist	All expenditures
Kansas	http://www.kssos.org/elections/elections_lobbyists.html	Client, lobbyist	Client names only
Kentucky	http://apps.klec.ky.gov/SearchRegister.asp	Client, lobbyist	Partial expenditures
Louisiana	http://ethics.la.gov/LobbyistData/SearchByCompRep.aspx	Client, lobbyist	Partial expenditures

Table A2.1 *Continued*

State	Website	Data Structure	Data Available
Maine	http://www.maine.gov/ethics/disclosure/lobbyists.htm	Client, lobbyist	All expenditures
Massachusetts	http://www.sec.state.ma.us/LobbyistPublicSearch/	Client, firm	All expenditures
Michigan	http://miboecfr.nictusa.com/cgi-bin/cfr/lobby_stats.cgi	Client	All expenditures
Minnesota	http://www.cfboard.state.mn.us/lob_lists.html	Client, lobbyist	Client names only
Mississippi	http://sos.ms.gov/elec/portal/msel/page/search/portal.aspx	Client, lobbyist	All expenditures
Missouri	http://mec.mo.gov/MEC/Lobbying/LB14_PrinExpSrch.aspx	Client, lobbyist	Partial expenditures
Montana	https://app.mt.gov/cgi-bin/camptrack/lobbysearch/lobbySearch.cgi	Client, lobbyist	All expenditures
Nebraska	http://nebraskalegislature.gov/lobbyist/view.php	Client, lobbyist	All expenditures
Nevada	https://www.leg.state.nv.us/AppCF/lobbyist/	Client, lobbyist	Client names only
New Hampshire	http://sos.nh.gov/LobReports.aspx	Client, lobbyist, firm	Client names only
New Jersey	http://www.elec.state.nj.us/publicinformation/gaa_annual.htm	Client, lobbyist, firm	All expenditures
New Mexico	https://www.cfis.state.nm.us/media/	Client	Partial expenditures
New York	https://onlineapps.jcope.ny.gov/LobbyWatch/Menu_reports_public.aspx	Client, firm	All expenditures
North Carolina	https://www.sosnc.gov/divisions/lobbying	Client, lobbyist	All expenditures
North Dakota	http://sos.nd.gov/lobbyists/registered-lobbyists	Client, lobbyist	Client names only
Ohio	http://www2.jlec-olig.state.oh.us/olac/	Client, lobbyist	Partial expenditures
Oklahoma	https://www.ok.gov/ethics/lobbyist/public_index.php	Client, lobbyist	Client names only

Continued

Table A2.1 *Continued*

State	Website	Data Structure	Data Available
Oregon	http://www.oregon.gov/ogec/pages/public_records.aspx	Client, lobbyist	All expenditures
Pennsylvania	https://www.palobbyingservices.state.pa.us/Public/wfSearch.aspx	Client, lobbyist	All expenditures
Rhode Island	https://www.lobbytracker.sos.ri.gov/Public/LobbyingReports.aspx	Client, lobbyist	Client names only
South Carolina	http://apps.sc.gov/LobbyingActivity/LAIndex.aspx	Client, lobbyist	All expenditures
South Dakota	https://sos.sd.gov/Lobbyist/LRPrintableList.aspx	Client, lobbyist	Client names only
Tennessee	https://apps.tn.gov/ilobbysearch-app/search.htm	Client, lobbyist	Partial expenditures
Texas	https://www.ethics.state.tx.us/	Client, lobbyist	All expenditures
Utah	http://lobbyist.utah.gov/Search/AdvancedSearch	Client	Client names only
Vermont	https://www.sec.state.vt.us/elections/lobbying/	Client, lobbyist	Partial expenditures
Virginia	https://solutions.virginia.gov/Lobbyist/Reports/Database	Client, lobbyist	All expenditures
Washington	https://www.pdc.wa.gov/browse/more-ways-to-follow-the-money/lobbying/agents?category=Lobbying	Client, lobbyist, firm	All expenditures
West Virginia	http://www.ethics.wv.gov/lobbyist/Pages/ListsandForms.aspx	Client, lobbyist	Client names only
Wisconsin	https://lobbying.wi.gov/Who/Principals/2015REG/SearchNames	Client, lobbyist	All expenditures
Wyoming	https://lobbyist.wyo.gov/Lobbyist/Default.aspx	Client, lobbyist	Client names only

Table A2.2 City Lobbying by State. Shows the years of available lobbying data, the number of cities with populations over 5,000, the percentage of cities that ever recorded lobbying activity, and descriptive statistics on lobbying expenditures for the states that disclose this information.

State	Years	# Cities	% Lobbying	Min Exp.	Median Exp.	Mean Exp.	Max Exp.
Alabama	2006–2015	101	35				
Alaska	2004–2015	11	64	1,778	40,000	38,737	62,543
Arizona	2000–2015	57	56	1,366	61,427	95,410	395,736
Arkansas	2006–2015	60	15				
California	2000–2015	426	65	1,246	40,000	65,555	1,773,094
Colorado	2002–2015	73	33	1,500	25,000	36,279	225,375
Connecticut	2006–2015	21	43	2,100	54,932	62,790	231,000
Delaware	2006–2015	10	20				
Florida	2006–2015	214	64	5,000	40,000	52,078	960,000
Georgia	2006–2015	121	24				
Hawaii	2000–2015	1	0				
Idaho	2000–2015	31	26				
Illinois	2006–2015	334	14				
Indiana	2006–2015	116	26	1,195	30,000	50,404	648,800
Iowa	2006–2015	77	18	2,000	28,183	52,491	758,731
Kansas	2006–2015	59	29				
Kentucky	2002–2015	74	8	1,427	8,010	8,432	17,800
Louisiana	2002–2015	63	21				
Maine	2006–2015	20	45	1,267	5,370	8,016	42,243
Maryland	2001–2015	39	33				
Massachusetts	2006–2015	53	4	16,012	24,700	31,353	60,000
Michigan	2001–2015	149	26	1,045	10,980	15,818	345,485
Minnesota	2000–2015	142	41				
Mississippi	2006–2015	64	23	8,000	30,000	39,498	146,000
Missouri	2002–2015	124	35				
Montana	2002–2015	16	44	1,500	13,562	16,428	41,682
Nebraska	2000–2015	33	24	4,200	34,744	43,249	110,610
Nevada	2006–2015	12	92				
New Hampshire	2005–2015	13	38				
New Jersey	2000–2015	194	7	304,000	440,000	440,000	576,000

Continued

Table A2.2 *Continued*

State	Years	# Cities	% Lobbying	Min Exp.	Median Exp.	Mean Exp.	Max Exp.
New Mexico	2002–2015	34	50				
New York	2000–2015	167	8	7,200	42,000	97,243	630,000
North Carolina	2005–2015	124	20	1,622	30,000	34,384	126,686
North Dakota	2006–2015	12	42				
Ohio	2006–2015	251	17				
Oklahoma	2006–2015	75	15				
Oregon	2000–2015	74	30	1,587	38,438	68,169	372,218
Pennsylvania	2000–2015	198	2	24,999	145,738	134,718	218,000
Rhode Island	2002–2015	8	50				
South Carolina	2006–2015	60	22	3,000	31,938	45,323	152,000
South Dakota	2006–2015	16	38				
Tennessee	2006–2015	95	20	20,000	47,500	47,667	100,000
Texas	2006–2015	334	44	5,000	50,000	96,412	1,130,000
Utah	2005–2015	81	9				
Vermont	2006–2015	8	38	9,634	20,166	20,166	30,698
Virginia	2002–2015	60	40	1,617	24,704	43,142	317,802
Washington	2000–2015	112	62	2,000	34,810	31,893	120,000
West Virginia	2005–2015	26	4				
Wisconsin	2006–2015	139	4	17,002	105,405	138,985	334,725
Wyoming	2000–2015	17	53				

City of Palo Alto   (ID # 4004)
CITY OF
PALO
ALTO   City Council Staff Report

Report Type: Consent Calendar   Meeting Date: 8/19/2013

Summary Title: State Lobbyist RFP

Title: Recommendation to Proceed with a Request for Proposals for State Legislative Advocacy and to Return to the Policy & Services Committee with a Recommendation on Final Contract Scope

From: City Manager

Lead Department: City Manager

Recommendation

1. Approve a recommendation from the Policy & Services Committee to hire a state lobbyist.

2. Approve the staff recommendation to issue a request for proposals (scope attached) for state legislative advocacy services and return to the Policy & Services Committee for direction on final contract scope of services.

Background

At the City Council's April 1 meeting, during its discussion of the 2013 Federal and State Legislative Program, the Council referred the issue of hiring a state lobbyist to the Policy & Services Committee. On April 9, during the Committee's discussion of its future meetings and agendas, the Committee agreed that the City Council consider hiring a state lobbyist without further discussion. This staff report provides an overview of the City's current federal and state legislative program and current agreements with lobbyists, and an overview of the plan and schedule for proceeding with a request for proposals for state legislative advocacy.

Discussion

The objective of the City of Palo Alto's legislative program, as defined in the Council approved Legislative Action Manual, is to keep the City Council, community and staff advised of proposed legislation with a potential impact upon the City. It is the City's general policy to take timely and effective action in support of, or opposition to, proposed legislation affecting Palo Alto at the county, state, and federal levels. In addition the City, where appropriate, seeks to take the

---

Figure A2.1 Palo Alto City Manager Report, August 2013. Report filed by the city manager enumerates the city's lobbying goals.

initiative to introduce new legislation beneficial to Palo Alto and other local government entities.

The groundwork for the City's legislative strategy is the Council's priorities. The City's five key guiding principles for legislative advocacy are as follows:

1. Protect local revenue sources and prevent unfunded mandates.

2. Protect and increase local government discretion, balancing that with City values and priorities.

3. Ensure that legislation, policies and budgets retain or increase, but generally don't decrease, the amount of local discretion held by the City and protect local decision making.

4. Oppose legislation, policies and budgets that reduce the authority and/or ability of local government to determine how best to effectively operate local programs, services and activities. The City retains the right to exceed State goals, standards or targets.

5. Protect and increase funding for specific programs and services.

6. Proactively advocate on behalf of the City.

7. Identify key legislative areas to monitor annually. Take a proactive role in working with Federal and State legislators to draft and sponsor legislation around key City priorities.

Each year, the Policy and Services Committee considers the City's general federal and state legislative program and priorities for the coming year and makes recommendations to the Council on adoption. The City also has legislative advocacy guidelines specific to utilities. Each year, the City's Utilities Advisory Committee also reviews the City's Utilities legislative advocacy guidelines and makes recommendations to the Council on adoption.

The City is represented and supported through several federal and state legislative advocacy sources. As illustrated below, at the federal level the City is supported on general matters by a contract lobbyist, Van Scoyoc Inc., and the National League of Cities. On technical matters relating to utility electric and water programs, compliance reporting and activities, and customer rates, the Northern California Power Agency (NCPA), American Public Power Association (APPA), California Municipal Utilities Association (CMUA), and the Bay Area Water Supply & Conservation Agency (BAWSCA) provide the City with legislative and regulatory support and representation. At the state level, the legislative program is largely managed by City staff, with support from the League of California Cities. The City is also supported at the state level on technical matters related to High Speed Rail and CEQA by the Professional Evaluation Group (PEG).

Figure A2.1 Continued

Chapter 3 Appendix

Table A3.1 shows summary statistics for all of the variables used throughout this chapter. The lobbying variables come from the original lobbying disclosure dataset described in detail in Chapter 2. *Population* and *own-source revenue* come from the Census of Governments and Survey of Local Government Finances. *Percent white*, *percent unemployed*, and *median home value* come from the American Community Survey. The *number of lower house representatives*, the *ideological distance* between representatives, and *delegation ideology score* come from Shor and McCarty (2015). *Democratic vote share* and *city ideology* come from Tausanovitch and Warshaw (2014). *Redistricted, Democratic City, Republican City*, and *Partisan Mismatch* are derived variables. Additional details can be found in the online replication files.

Table A3.2 shows the correlates of city lobbying from a pooled OLS model with either state or state by year fixed effects. Predicted values from the first column are plotted against observed values of covariates in Figure 3.1 and Figure 3.2 in the main text.

Table A3.1 Summary Statistics.

Statistic	Obs.	Mean	St. Dev.	Min	Max
Lobby	57,716	0.16	0.37	0	1
Lobby Expenditures	4,773	60,126	104,099	1,045	1,773,094
Population	57,716	39,011	177,688	1,792	8,550,405
Median Income	57,585	55,738	25,609	13,149	250,000
Own-Source Revenue (Log)	54,536	7.14	0.69	0.30	11.66
% White	57,585	78.30	18.30	0.40	100.00
% Unemployed	57,584	5.48	2.30	0.20	22.60
Median Home Value	57,585	232,807	186,422	32,600	2,000,000
# Lower House Representatives	54,456	1.79	2.04	1.00	67.00
Ideological Distance Between Reps	49,225	0.31	0.63	0.00	6.11
Redistricted	54,456	0.16	0.37	0.00	1.00
Delegation Ideology Score	49,225	0.08	0.95	−3.04	3.71
Democratic Vote Share (2008)	14,314	0.59	0.15	0.22	0.99
City Ideology Score	15,887	−0.07	0.26	−1.02	0.65
Democratic City	6,875	0.49	0.50	0.00	1.00
Republican City	6,875	0.51	0.50	0.00	1.00
Partisan Mismatch	6,122	0.09	0.29	0.00	1.00

Table A3.2 Correlates of City Lobbying.

	Probability of Lobbying	
	(1)	(2)
# House Representatives	0.003*	0.003*
	(0.001)	(0.001)
Ideological Distance	0.027*	0.027*
	(0.003)	(0.003)
Population (Log)	0.140*	0.140*
	(0.002)	(0.002)
% White	−0.001*	−0.001*
	(0.0001)	(0.0001)
Median Income (Log)	0.578*	0.596*
	(0.141)	(0.141)
Median Income Squared (Log)	−0.027*	−0.028*
	(0.006)	(0.006)
Own-Source Revenue (Log)	0.025*	0.025*
	(0.002)	(0.002)
Median House Value (Log)	0.014*	0.016*
	(0.005)	(0.005)
State FEs	Yes	
Year FEs	Yes	
State-Year FEs		Yes
Observations	49,186	49,186
# Cities	4,599	4,599
Mean Lobbying Probability	0.16	0.16

Pooled cross-sectional models estimated by OLS. Robust standard errors clustered by city. *p<0.05

Difference-in-Differences Estimation

The main empirical strategy used throughout this chapter is a two-way fixed effects or generalized difference-in-differences approach. To obtain within-city estimates of various treatments on the probability of lobbying, I estimate equations of the following form:

$$Lobby_{it} = \beta_1 Treat_{it} + X'_{it}\beta_2 + \gamma_i + \eta_t + \epsilon_{it},$$

where $Lobby_{it}$ equals one if city i disclosed lobbying activity in year t. The coefficient of interest is β_1, which captures the effect of the treatment of interest on the probability of lobbying (for example, being redistricted, an election leading to a partisan mismatch, or an election that changes the ideological composition of a city's delegation). X_{it} include time-varying combinations of the city-level covariates described in Section 3.3. City fixed effects are captured by γ_i and adjust for time-invariant characteristics that might influence a city's demand for lobbying from year to year. Finally, η_t include either year or state-by-year fixed effects and account for temporal shocks like the Great Recession that might broadly increase or decrease lobbying by all cities in given period. State-year fixed effects provide the most stringent tests, but they also use up significantly more degrees of freedom. When I perform subset analyses and the number of cities drops into the low hundreds, I generally prefer to include year fixed effects (rather than state-year), because there simply aren't enough cities per state to draw effective comparisons.

Redistricting Analysis

Table A3.3 presents the difference-in-differences estimates for the effect of being redistricted in 2010 in a way that increased the size of a city's delegation. Columns 1–3 display the results for all cities in the sample with a population over 5,000, and columns 4–6 show the results for large cities with a population over 100,000. Gaining representatives through redistricting increases the probability of lobbying for all cities by around 3 percentage points. Note that the inclusion of state-by-year fixed effects washes away much of this effect in the full sample, suggesting that particular states might be driving this result. However, for the larger sample of cities, the effect of redistricting remains fairly constant across specifications.

Table A3.3 Effect of Gaining Representatives after Redistricting on City Lobbying.

	Probability of Lobbying					
	Population > 5,000			Population > 100,000		
	(1)	(2)	(3)	(4)	(5)	(6)
Redistricted	0.036*	0.028*	0.012	0.084*	0.091*	0.076*
	(0.011)	(0.011)	(0.011)	(0.035)	(0.035)	(0.038)
City FEs	Yes	Yes	Yes	Yes	Yes	Yes
Year FEs	Yes	Yes		Yes	Yes	
State-Year FEs			Yes			Yes
Full Controls		Yes	Yes		Yes	Yes
Observations	57,716	54,445	54,445	3,536	3,296	3,296
# Cities	4,599	4,590	4,590	275	274	274
Mean Lobbying Probability	0.16	0.16	0.16	0.72	0.73	0.73

Full controls include log population, log median income, log own-source revenue per capita, and log median house value. Robust standard errors clustered by city. *p<0.05

Partisanship and Ideology Analysis

Table A3.4 presents the differences-in-differences estimates for the effect of a city becoming mismatched with its lower state delegation. The sample for this analysis comprises cities with a population over 20,000, which is the set of cities for which partisanship and ideology estimates exist (Tausanovitch and Warshaw 2014). Republican cities are defined as those in the bottom tercile of Democratic vote share in 2008 and the most conservative tercile of Tausanovitch and Warshaw ideology scores. Democratic cities are those in the top tercile of Democratic vote share and the most liberal third of the ideology scores. A mismatch occurs when an election leads more than 50 percent of a city's delegation to come from the opposite party. Note that moderate cities aren't included in this analysis, as it's difficult to determine whether such cities are aligned or mismatched with their delegations. The results in Table A3.4 indicate that cities are around 5 percentage points more likely to lobby after a partisan mismatch occurs with their delegation. These results remain very stable across specifications.

I perform several robustness checks to ensure the validity of the difference-in-differences design. The key assumption of this approach is that aligned and mismatched cities would have followed the same lobbying trend if the mismatched cities had not elected a non-aligned candidate. Recently, a variety of new approaches have been introduced to improve difference-in-difference estimation with more than two groups and treatment periods (e.g., Goodman-Bacon 2018; De Chaisemartin and d'Haultfoeuille 2018). To probe the parallel trends assumption, I follow the framework introduce by Liu, Wang, and Xu (2020) and use their R package, "A Practical Guide to Counterfactual Estimators for Causal Inference with Time-Series Cross-Sectional Data." Figure A3.1 shows the counterfactual estimators for several years before and after treatment. There do not appear to be any concerning pre-treatment trends, and the increase in lobbying occurs only after a city's delegation flips party. I also perform the standard test of leads and lags (Angrist and Pischke 2008). These results closely mirror the counterfactual estimates in Figure A3.1 and are available in the online replication files.

Table A3.4 Effect of Delegation Mismatch on City Lobbying.

	Probability of Lobbying			
	(1)	(2)	(3)	(4)
Partisan Mismatch	0.051*	0.056*	0.050*	0.056*
	(0.020)	(0.020)	(0.023)	(0.023)
City FEs	Yes	Yes	Yes	Yes
Year FEs	Yes	Yes		
State-Year FEs			Yes	Yes
Full Controls		Yes		Yes
Observations	5,887	5,877	5,887	5,877
# Cities	531	531	531	531
Mean Lobbying Probability	0.48	0.48	0.48	0.48

Full controls include log population, log median income, log own-source revenue per capita, and log median house value. Robust standard errors clustered by city. *$p<0.05$

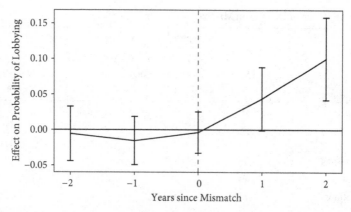

Figure A3.1 Effect of Becoming Mismatched with State Delegation: Leads and Lags. Counterfactual estimates produced by the fect package in R (Liu, Wang, and Xu 2019).

Table A3.5 Effect of Partisan Mismatch on Lobbying by City Size.

	Probability of Lobbying			
	Full Sample	Population 20,000–50,000	Population 50,000–100,000	Population Over 100,000
	(1)	(2)	(3)	(4)
Partisan Mismatch	0.056*	0.067*	0.104*	−0.033
	(0.020)	(0.030)	(0.043)	(0.019)
City FEs	Yes	Yes	Yes	Yes
Year FEs	Yes	Yes	Yes	Yes
Full Controls	Yes	Yes	Yes	Yes
Observations	5,877	2,392	2,064	1,421
# Cities	531	222	182	127
Mean Lobbying Probability	0.48	0.3	0.48	0.77

Full controls include log population, log median income, log own-source revenue per capita, and log median house value. Robust standard errors clustered by city. *$p<0.05$

Table A3.5 examines how the effect of a partisan mismatch varies across cities of different sizes. Mid-sized municipalities with between 50,000 and 100,000 residents are particularly sensitive to the partisan composition of their delegation and subsequently increase their probability of disclosing lobbying activity by 10 percentage points. Large cities with over 100,000 residents don't appear to be more likely to lobby following a mismatch with their delegation—but note that their probability of lobbying is already quite high (77%). In Table A3.6, I find that large cities dramatically increase their *spending* on lobbying in response to partisan mismatches in the twenty-seven states for which expenditure data exist (see Chapter 2 for discussion of these states). The outcome is log transformed, so the coefficient of 0.681 translates into nearly a 100 percent increase in spending ($exp(0.681) - 1 \times 100 = 97.48$). Cities over this population threshold spend

Table A3.6 Effect of Delegation Mismatch on Lobbying Expenditures.

	Expenditures on Lobbying (Log)			
	Full Sample (1)	Population 20,000–50,000 (2)	Population 50,000–100,000 (3)	Population Over 100,000 (4)
Partisanship Mismatch	0.635* (0.323)	0.049 (0.788)	0.822 (0.495)	0.681* (0.284)
City FEs	Yes	Yes	Yes	Yes
State-Year FEs	Yes	Yes	Yes	Yes
Full Controls	Yes	Yes	Yes	Yes
Observations	4,251	1,029	1,614	1,608
# Cities	547	165	205	177
Mean Log Exp.	7.12	6.08	7.42	7.48

Full controls include log population, log median income, log own-source revenue per capita, and log median house value. Robust standard errors clustered by city. *$p<0.05$

Table A3.7 Effect of Delegation Partisanship vs. Ideology on City Lobbying.

	Probability of Lobbying					
	Democratic City			Republican City		
	(1)	(2)	(3)	(4)	(5)	(6)
Partisan Mismatch	0.064* (0.028)		0.038 (0.026)	0.059 (0.031)		0.067* (0.034)
Conservative Ideology		0.031* (0.014)	0.036* (0.015)		0.006 (0.016)	0.014 (0.014)
City FEs	Yes	Yes	Yes	Yes	Yes	Yes
Year FEs	Yes	Yes	Yes	Yes	Yes	Yes
Full Controls	Yes	Yes	Yes	Yes	Yes	Yes
Observations	2,867	2,958	2,724	3,010	2,955	2,697
# Cities	246	245	245	285	281	281
Mean Lobbying Probability	0.53	0.52	0.52	0.43	0.43	0.44

Full controls include log population, log median income, log own-source revenue per capita, and log median house value. Robust standard errors clustered by city. *$p<0.05$

$106,018 on average for their lobbying contracts each year, so doubling this amount would result in net expenditures of over $200,000.

Next, I break down the response to partisan mismatches by Republican and Democratic cities. Both types of cities are about equally likely to increase their lobbying rates in response to their delegation flipping parties (columns 1 and 4 of Table A3.7). I also examine how the propensity to lobby changes in response to shifts in the ideological composition of the state delegation, after accounting for partisanship. Legislator ideology scores are estimated by Shor and McCarty and range from −2.667 (most liberal) to 3.272 (most conservative) over the course of the panel. With this analysis, I find some important distinctions between Republican and Democratic cities.

For Democratic cities, the effect of partisan mismatches appears to be driven in large part because these mismatches result in delegations that are more conservative. When measures of both partisanship and ideology are included in the same model, the effect of delegation ideology dominates. However, the same is not true for Republican cities. Republican cities are more likely to lobby when their delegation is majority Democratic— but they are not more likely to lobby as the delegation becomes more liberal. If any-thing, column 6 indicates that Republican cities are also a bit more likely to lobby as their delegations become more conservative (although the effect is much weaker than that for Democratic cities).

Finally, I examine how partisan mismatches with the lower legislative chamber affect the probability of city lobbying. Is there something special about a city's relationship to its district representatives, or does the partisan composition of the chamber as a whole also matter? Table A3.8 shows that a city's partisan alignment with district representatives has a larger and more precisely estimated effect on lobbying than alignment with the lower house more generally. The variable *Chamber Mismatch* takes a value of 1 when members of the opposite party comprise a majority in the lower house. Cities are more likely to dis-close lobbying activity after their delegation flips, relative to the entire chamber.

Table A3.8 Effect of Delegation vs. Chamber Mismatch on City Lobbying.

	Probability of Lobbying	
	(1)	(2)
Chamber Mismatch	0.025	0.021
	(0.029)	(0.028)
Delegation Mismatch		0.056*
		(0.022)
City FEs	Yes	Yes
State-Year FEs	Yes	Yes
Full Controls	Yes	Yes
Observations	6,350	5,825
# Cities	527	527
Mean Lobbying Probability	0.48	0.48

Full controls include log population, log median income, log own-source revenue per capita, and log median house value. Robust standard errors clustered by city. *p<0.05

Chapter 4 Appendix

Table A4.1 shows how rates of city mobilization vary across states based on several fixed geographic and institutional traits. A higher percentage of cities lobby in states with both term limits and greater legislative professionalism. These two factors also predict cities comprising a larger proportion of all interest groups. Figure 4.4 in the main text shows the predicted values from column 2.

Table A4.2 demonstrates that the political correlates of lobbying across states (column 1) generally fail to explain within-state mobilization (column 2). One exception is the share of state transfers comprising city budgets. As state transfers make up a larger share of city budgets, a higher proportion of cities disclose lobbying activity both across states and within states over time. A 10 percentage point increase in the share of state transfers as a percent of city budgets is associated with a 2.5 percentage point increase in mobilization rates. Finally, Figure A4.1 depicts the percent of cities lobbying over time in each state. While some states tend to have the same number of cities lobbying every year, other states experience dramatic jumps in the amount of municipal lobbying from year to year.

Table A4.1 Geographic and Institutional Correlates of City Lobbying across States.

	% Cities Lobbying		Cities as % of All IGs (2007)
	(1)	(2)	(3)
Total Cities	0.012	−0.014	0.007*
	(0.009)	(0.009)	(0.002)
Average City Population (Log)	6.348*	6.244*	0.172
	(0.938)	(0.903)	(0.222)
Cities per Thousand Square Miles	−0.428*	−0.211	−0.065
	(0.148)	(0.146)	(0.038)
Term Limits	7.733*	−6.201*	−1.524*
	(1.357)	(2.395)	(0.574)
Legislative Professionalism	−19.113*	−39.835*	−4.148*
	(7.168)	(7.518)	(1.777)
Term Limits × Leg Prof		68.887*	10.069*
		(9.923)	(2.483)
Year FEs	Yes	Yes	
Observations	620	620	50
# States	50	50	50
Mean DV	16.1	16.1	1.2

Pooled cross-sectional models estimated by OLS. Robust standard errors clustered by state in Models 1 and 2. *p<0.05

Table A4.2 Political Correlates of City Lobbying across States.

	% Cities Lobbying	
	(1)	(2)
Republican Governor	2.962*	−0.553
	(1.241)	(0.616)
Proportion House Republicans	4.493	−5.885
	(4.416)	(4.545)
Divided Government	2.582*	0.288
	(1.241)	(0.559)
House Polarization	10.318*	−4.161*
	(1.137)	(2.083)
State Transfers as % of City Budgets	0.299*	0.255*
	(0.059)	(0.114)
Average City Population (Log)	6.368*	12.503
	(0.977)	(7.054)
Year FEs	Yes	Yes
State FEs		Yes
Observations	534	534
# States	50	50
Mean DV	16.1	16.1

Robust standard errors clustered by state. *p<0.05

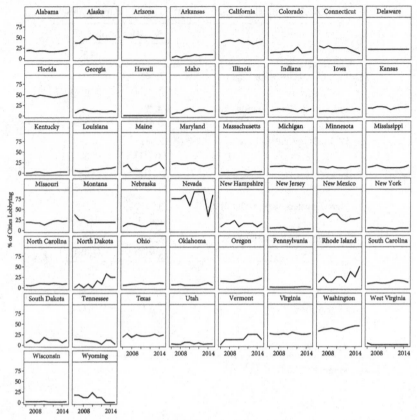

Figure A4.1 Within-State Changes in City Lobbying, 2006–2015. Shows rates of within-state lobbying over time.

Chapter 5 Appendix

To examine the returns to city lobbying, I estimate regressions of the following form via OLS:

$$State\ Transfers_{ijt} = \beta_1 Lobby_{ijt} + X_{ijt}'\beta_2 + \gamma_i + \eta_{jt} + \epsilon_{ijt}$$

where $State\ Transfers_{ijt}$ is the funding that city i receives from state j in year t. I generally present results in terms of per capita state transfers, although I get a similar pattern of findings using logged state transfers as the outcome. The coefficient of interest is β_1, which captures the average effect of city i's decision to lobby on the state revenue it receives that year. City fixed effects are represented by γ_i; η_{jt} are either year or state-year fixed effects, and ϵ_{it} are individual disturbances. The city fixed effects control for any time invariant local characteristics that might influence both municipal lobbying and state funding, while the state-year fixed effects adjust for state and year specific shocks to municipal transfers. The standard errors presented in the following results are always clustered at the city level to correct for correlation across within-city error terms over time. In certain specifications, I also include various combinations of city-level covariates, which are represented by X_{ijt}. The full models adjust for the following: population, median income, own-source revenue, percent white, and median home values. While there are many potential variables that could be added to the models, these controls capture a range of economic and demographic indicators and are among the best predictors of state funding. Table A5.1 shows how these variables correlate with state transfers per capita from pooled OLS models.

Table A5.2 shows the results from the difference-in-differences analysis with city and year fixed effects. Cities can expect to receive around $8 to $10 more capita after they lobby compared to other cities. Table A5.3 breaks down the effect of lobbying by city size. Mid-sized cities with between 50,000 and 100,000 residents do particularly well when they lobby, but cities of all sizes experience positive returns, on average.

I also replicate the main analyses using logged total state transfers as the outcome variable instead of state transfers per capita. The results follow a very similar pattern and suggest that cities get around 5 percent more revenue from the state after lobbying (Table A5.4). In the online replication files, I show that the main results are also robust to dropping outliers and to subsetting to the group of cities with complete financial data available in the Survey of Local Government Finances.

Table A5.1 Correlates of State Transfers to Cities.

	State Transfers (per Capita)	
	(1)	(2)
Lobby	23.038*	23.951*
	(5.504)	(5.468)
Population (Log)	−30.839*	−32.220*
	(3.538)	(3.507)
Median Income (Log)	−156.937*	−146.590*
	(9.529)	(9.451)
Own-Source Revenue (Log)	69.188*	69.167*
	(2.787)	(2.765)
% White	−1.684*	−1.618*
	(0.130)	(0.128)
Median House Value (Log)	25.710*	11.009
	(8.515)	(8.647)
% College Degree	−1.144*	−0.895*
	(0.215)	(0.214)
State FEs	Yes	
Year FEs	Yes	
State-Year FEs		Yes
Observations	32,112	32,112
# Cities	4,589	4,589
Mean Transfer	275.1	275.1

Robust standard errors clustered by city. *p<0.05

Table A5.2 Effect of Lobbying on State Transfers.

	State Transfers (per Capita)			
	(1)	(2)	(3)	(4)
Lobby	10.880*	9.824*	8.678	8.208
	(5.121)	(5.008)	(4.971)	(4.93)
City FEs	Yes	Yes	Yes	Yes
Year FEs	Yes	Yes		
State-Year FEs			Yes	Yes
Full Controls		Yes		Yes
Observations	32,148	32,112	32,148	32,112
# Cities	4,593	4,589	4,593	4,589
Mean Transfer	274.9	275.1	274.9	275.1

Full controls include log population, log median income, log own-source revenue, log median house value, and % white. Robust standard errors clustered by city. *p<0.05

Table A5.3 Effect of Lobbying on State Transfers by City Size.

	State Transfers (per Capita)			
	Full Sample (1)	Under 50,000 (2)	50,000–100,000 (3)	Over 100,000 (4)
Lobby	10.880*	6.888	18.723*	12.006
	(5.121)	(7.514)	(7.868)	(8.629)
City FEs	Yes	Yes	Yes	Yes
Year FEs	Yes	Yes	Yes	Yes
Observations	32,148	24,681	4,231	3,236
# Cities	4,593	3,889	429	275
Mean Transfer	274.9	248	334.1	403.2

Full controls include log population, log median income, log own-source revenue, log median house value, and % white. Robust standard errors clustered by city. *p<0.05

Table A5.4 Effect of Lobbying on State Transfers (Logged).

	State Transfers (Logged)			
	Full Sample (1)	Under 50,000 (2)	50,000–100,000 (3)	Over 100,000 (4)
Lobby	0.050	0.049	0.077*	0.024
	(0.040)	(0.055)	(0.035)	(0.134)
City FEs	Yes	Yes	Yes	Yes
Year FEs	Yes	Yes	Yes	Yes
Observations	30,563	23,462	4,028	3,073
# Cities	4,593	3,889	429	275
Mean Transfers per Capita	14.9	14.3	16.1	17.4

Models control for log population. Robust standard errors clustered by city. *p<0.05

Parallel Trends

In the main text, Figure 5.3 shows the pre-treatment trends for cities that started lobbying in 2012 or 2013 compared to non-lobbying cities for the subset of cities with complete financial data available via the Survey of Local Government Finances. In Table A5.5, I include leads and lags of the lobbying treatment variable in a regression framework that includes all municipalities with at least five observations in the Survey of Government Data. While this analysis is somewhat noisy given the short nature of the panel, the coefficients on the lead variables are small and not statistically distinguishable from zero.

Because the Survey of Government Finances draws from a sample of municipalities in most years, I also replicate this analysis for the complete set of cities with a population over 1,000 in California, Washington, and Florida. These states provide complete financial data for their municipalities, allowing me to ensure that the results are robust to using multiple datasets and aren't being driven by the sampling procedure used by the Survey of Government Finances. Table A5.6 shows these results. Again, the coefficients on the leads of the treatment are all small and not precisely estimated.

Table A5.5 City Lobbying and State Transfers: Lags and Leads.

	State Transfers (per Capita)				
	(1)	(2)	(3)	(4)	(5)
Lobby, $t + 2$					2.576
					(4.401)
Lobby, $t + 1$		0.747	3.408	2.339	0.414
		(3.902)	(3.976)	(4.095)	(4.780)
Lobby, t	8.309*	7.935*	5.698	5.880	7.231
	(3.379)	(3.903)	(4.411)	(4.475)	(4.744)
Lobby, $t - 1$			1.225	−1.807	0.040
			(3.934)	(4.430)	(4.694)
Lobby, $t - 2$				6.893	5.858
				(4.050)	(4.380)
City FEs	Yes	Yes	Yes	Yes	Yes
Year FEs	Yes	Yes	Yes	Yes	Yes
Observations	25,499	25,499	23,796	21,626	19,435
# Cities	2,841	2,841	2,840	2,839	2,839
Mean Transfers per Capita	250.7	250.7	249	247.9	247.9

Models control for population. Robust standard errors clustered by city. *$p<0.05$

Table A5.6 Lags and Leads: California, Washington, and Florida

	State Transfers (per Capita), $t + 1$				
	(1)	(2)	(3)	(4)	(5)
Lobby, $t + 2$					3.374
					(5.620)
Lobby, $t + 1$		2.072	−1.333	−1.846	−2.823
		(8.224)	(7.670)	(7.202)	(5.825)
Lobby, t	16.982*	15.891*	16.692*	16.587*	15.143*
	(6.753)	(6.978)	(6.596)	(6.655)	(6.433)
Lobby, $t - 1$			1.784	−2.843	−1.906
			(4.399)	(4.141)	(4.162)
Lobby, $t - 2$				7.334	6.996
				(4.051)	(4.187)
City FEs	Yes	Yes	Yes	Yes	Yes
Year FEs	Yes	Yes	Yes	Yes	Yes
Observations	8,049	8,049	7,737	7,625	7,477
# Cities	912	878	878	876	876

Models control for population. Robust standard errors clustered by city. *p<0.05

Additional Results

Next, I use the same difference-in-differences framework to examine if changes in lobbying expenditures lead cities to capture more state revenue. For this analysis, I rely on the set of twenty-seven states with complete expenditure data available (see Chapter 2 for details). Using the same estimating equation but replacing the lobbying indicator with a measure of lobbying spending per capita, I find that each additional dollar invested in lobbying substantially increases the size of the state transfer. This result remains consistent across cities of all sizes (Table A5.7).

Finally, I examine how the success of lobbying varies by city income. Table A5.8 shows the result from a model including a continuous interaction between city median income and the lobbying indicator. Each 10 percent increase in median income is associated with receiving just under $4 more per capita in state transfers following the decision to lobby ($40.26 \times log(1.10) = 3.84$). Results follow a nearly identical pattern when breaking cities into terciles based on their median incomes (see the online replication files).

Table A5.7 Effect of Lobbying Expenditures on State Transfers.

	State Transfers (per Capita)			
	Full Sample (1)	Under 50,000 (2)	50,000–100,000 (3)	Over 100,000 (4)
Lobby Expenditures (Per Capita)	8.381* (3.615)	5.795 (4.835)	9.739 (7.666)	8.778* (4.093)
City FEs	Yes	Yes	Yes	Yes
State-Year FEs	Yes	Yes	Yes	Yes
Observations	4,728	1,637	1,369	1,788
# Cities	888	500	217	183
Mean Transfers	191.8	282.3	167.8	180.1

Models control for population. Robust standard errors clustered by city. *p<0.05

Table A5.8 Effect of Lobbying on State Transfers by Median Income .

	State Transfers (per Capita)	
	(1)	(2)
Lobby× Median Income (Log)	45.121* (14.108)	40.259* (13.494)
City FEs	Yes	Yes
Year FEs	Yes	
State-Year FEs		Yes
Full Controls	Yes	Yes
Observations	22,361	22,361
# Cities	3,204	3,204

Full controls include log population, log median income, log own-source revenue, log median house value, and % white. Robust standard errors clustered by city. *p<0.05

Chapter 6 Appendix

Table A6.1 shows that as more cities within a state disclose lobbying activity, high-income cities capture a greater overall share of state transfers, making the transfer system less progressive. Predicted values from column 2 are shown in Figure 6.3 in the main text. A 10 percent increase in the number of cities lobbying is associated with a 3 percent increase in total transfers to cities in the top third of the income distribution. Table A6.2 shows that this effect only occurs after cities mobilize and not before.

Table A6.1 Effect of Lobbying on Share of State Transfers to High-Income Cities.

	Share Transfers to High-Income Cities	
	(1)	(2)
Proportion Cities Lobbying	0.212*	0.314*
	(0.105)	(0.130)
State FEs	Yes	Yes
Year FEs	Yes	Yes
States with > 15 Cities		Yes
Observations	376	336
Mean Share to High-Income Cities	0.31	0.3

Models control for the party of the governor, the proportion of the lower house controlled by Democrats, and total state expenditures. Robust standard errors clustered by state. *p<0.05

Table A6.2 Effect of Lobbying on Share of State Transfers to High-Income Cities: Leads and Lags

	Share Transfers to High-Income Cities	
	All States	States with > 15 Cities
	(1)	(2)
Proportion Cities Lobbying, t − 1	0.025	0.074
	(0.143)	(0.179)
Proportion Cities Lobbying, t	0.212	0.300
	(0.121)	(0.161)
Proportion Cities Lobbying, t + 1	0.077	0.083
	(0.117)	(0.147)
State FEs	Yes	Yes
Year FEs	Yes	Yes
Observations	288	258
Mean Share to High-Income Cities	0.31	0.3

Robust standard errors clustered by state. *p<0.05

Notes

Chapter 1

1. Brenan (2017).
2. Nidever (2015).
3. Census of Governments (2012), "Individual State Descriptions." *United States Census Bureau*, https://www.census.gov/content/dam/Census/library/publications/2012/econ/2012isd.pdf.

Chapter 2

1. Finch (1925).
2. Beard (1913).
3. Examples include Cammisa (1995), Flanagan (1999), and Cigler (2012). Two notable recent advances in this literature are Loftis and Kettler (2015) and Goldstein and You (2017), who study the lobbying decisions of individual city governments. Loftis and Kettler find that local unemployment rates correlate with a city's decision to lobby in Washington, DC, and Goldstein and You use over a decade of disclosure data to demonstrate that cities lobby the federal government when they have incongruent ideological preferences with their state governments, which they argue leads to an under provision of local public goods. For an excellent review of the scholarship on intergovernmental lobbying, see Jensen (2019).
4. For a thorough overview, see De Figueiredo and Richter (2014).
5. 2 U.S.C. § 1602(8)(A).
6. See https://www.ncsl.org/research/ethics/50-state-chart-lobbyist-report.-requirements.aspx for a more detailed discussion of disclosure standards by state.
7. Britschgi (2017).
8. Interview with the author, Sept. 19, 2017.
9. Interview with the author, March 4, 2021.
10. https://www.census.gov/govs/cog/about_the_data.html.
11. I chose to focus on cities with at least 5,000 residents because below this threshold, the scope and responsibilities of municipal government fall dramatically, and very little lobbying takes place.
12. Notable exceptions include De Soto (1995); Freeman and Nownes (1999); Weir, Wolman, and Swanstrom (2005); Lowery et al. (2012).

13. https://www.urban.org/policy-centers/cross-center-initiatives/state-and-local-finance-initiative/state-and-local-backgrounders/state-and-local-revenues.

14. Radnofsky and Eaton (2009).

15. Ogorzalek (2018) provides an in-depth treatment of how cities have shaped national politics over the course of the twentieth century.

16. https://clerk.assembly.ca.gov/sites/clerk.assembly.ca.gov/files/archive/DailyJournal/1951/Volumes/51_jnl_vol4.PDF.

17. See Drutman (2015) for a discussion of the evolution of the corporate lobbying industry in Washington, DC.

18. Doughman (2013).

19. Office of the Legislative Auditor, State of Minnesota (1990), "Local Government Lobbying," http://www.auditor.leg.state.mn.us/ped/1990/90-02.pdf.

20. Herdt (1997), "Counties, Cities Pay Big Bucks to Lobby." *Ventura County Star*, December 29: A-1.

21. Interview with the author, March 4, 2021.

22. Harrie (2015).

23. Gonsalves (2002), 135.

24. Interview with the author, March 5, 2021.

25. Interview with the author, March 4, 2021.

26. Of course, interest groups of all types employ lobbyists to perform similar functions. Rosenthal (1993), Nownes (2006), Hrebenar and Morgan (2009), LaPira and Thomas (2017), and others describe the mechanics of the lobbying process more generally in great detail. In Chapter 3, I turn to the question of how and why local governments are different from other types of organizations that lobby.

27. https://www.tml.org/DocumentCenter/View/798/2015-to-2016-Legislative-Policy-Development-Process-PDF.

28. DuPuis et al. (2018).

29. Interview with the author, March 11, 2021.

30. Rosenthal (1993).

31. Interview with the author, April 8, 2021.

32. McGreevy and Willon (2015).

33. Rudoren and Pilhofer (2006).

34. Rudoren and Pilhofer (2006).

35. https://www.townsendpa.com/portfolio-items/local-government/.

36. https://www.cityofsacramento.org/-/media/Corporate/Files/CMO/Intergovernmental-Relations/2018-Legislative-Platform_041018-revisions.pdf?la=en.

37. Finke (2013).

38. http://legacy.elpasotexas.gov/muni_clerk/agenda/09-27-11/09271113B.pdf.

39. https://www.rockvillemd.gov/DocumentCenter/View/28369/RFP-06-19-State-Lobbying-and-Legislative-Representation-Services?bidId=.

40. Spector (2014).

41. Interview with the author, March 11, 2021.

42. http://www.jcope.ny.gov/view_filing.html.

43. Finke (2013).
44. De Soto (1995).
45. Interview with the author, March 11, 2021.
46. Interview with the author, March 4, 2021.

Chapter 3

1. The American Conservative Union, "2011 State Legislative Ratings Guide: North Carolina," http://acuratings.conservative.org/wp-content/uploads/sites/5/2015/01/126321852-2011-North- Carolina-State-Legislative-Ratings.pdf.
2. Interview with the author, April 8, 2021.
3. To be clear, the notion of "city size" is bundled with many other local conditions. Big cities are home to more residents, but they also typically have higher rates of inequality and poverty, provide more municipal services, employ larger city staffs, etc. It is likely the each of these factors—as well as their interaction—contributes to the demand for lobbying.
4. Note that across cities of all types, white, affluent, and educated individuals are often more likely to vote and thus to exert disproportionate influence over local elections (see Hajnal and Trounstine [2005] for a review). However, in places where these individuals make up a larger share of residents, the incentives to cater to this demographic should also increase.
5. At the same time, private interests lack the natural built-in representation that local governments enjoy. As Jason Gonsalves told me, "Private clients have to find their niche and identify the issues based on the political landscape. Private clients don't have 'their' member of the legislature per se. You don't have the natural relationships that mayors and city councils may have with their district legislators." (Interview with the author, March 4, 2021.)
6. Interview with the author, March 5, 2021.
7. Interview with the author, Sept. 19, 2017.
8. Longley (2011).
9. Finke (2013).
10. Herz (2016).
11. Humphrey (2014).
12. Rudoren and Pilhofer (2006).
13. Coolican (2016).
14. Harrie (2015).
15. Interview with the author, Sept. 19, 2017.
16. Radelat (2015).
17. Interview with the author, April 8, 2021.
18. Interview with the author, May 11, 2018.
19. I merged this information with the city-level data by relying on geocodes provided by the Missouri Census Center. Critically, this mapping from state legislative districts to

cities is available before and after the 2010 census redistricting, which allowed me to accurately place cities throughout the course of the panel (which runs from 2006 to 2015 for all states and back to 2000 for certain states. See the appendix to Chapter 2 for additional details).

20. It's also important to note that cities aren't lobbying in a vacuum. They may be joined (or opposed) by their surrounding counties, special districts, local business organizations, or other interest groups. Unfortunately, there is just no way to know for certain which local interests are mobilizing alongside the thousands of municipalities in my dataset. Dana Fenton of Charlotte told me that when he was seeking funding for the city's light rail system, UNC Charlotte and the business community actively partnered with the city to advocate for the project (interview with the author, April 8, 2021). I assume that if city official could simply rely on other actors in the region to lobby for them, they would. As long as some randomness exists in the particular constellation of local interests that are choosing to lobby in a particular region, then any measurement error introduced by the inability to quantify this activity should serve to attenuate the results.

21. Additional details and the regression results are in the chapter appendix.

22. I discuss the Shor and McCarty ideology scores in a bit more detail in the following section. A greater distance between scores indicates more ideological division in roll call votes, which might also be thought of as a measure of polarization.

23. Simon (2009).

24. Finke (2013).

25. For details on the estimation and formal results, see the chapter appendix.

26. KCET (2011).

27. This analysis can also be thought of as a placebo test, and results are available in the online replication files.

28. Marin (2017).

29. Interview with the author, March 5, 2021.

30. Similarly, Lowery (2007) points out that many of the day-to-day interactions between lobbyists and government officials don't involve major policy battles but instead might better be described as "casework."

31. Craver (2019).

32. Freer (2019).

33. Interview with the author, April 8, 2021.

34. Specifically, the authors employ multilevel regression with post-stratification (MRP) to generate city ideal points, which they validate at length in Tausanovitch and Warshaw (2014).

35. This approach is similar to Einstein and Kogan (2016), who demonstrate that average partisan preferences across cities correlate with municipal spending. Of course, there are other ways that one might classify the partisan tendencies of cities. Gerber and Hopkins (2011), for example, show that Republican and Democratic mayors diverge somewhat in their budgeting choices over certain policies. In Payson (2020b), I use data collected by de Benedictis-Kessner (2018) to show that the party of the mayor correlates strongly with my measure of city partisanship for a subset of cities.

Because so many cities in my sample have nonpartisan elections, here I choose to focus on city vote share and resident ideology to classify cities—rather than mayoral partisanship—in order to maximize the sample size.

36. Note that this is the same basic setup that I employed in Payson (2020b), but with several additional years of data.

37. For a more formal discussion of the estimation strategy, see the chapter appendix.

38. For more technical details, see the chapter appendix.

39. See the Chapter 2 appendix for details on the states with expenditure information available.

40. While not extremely common, there were 113 observations of such partisan mismatches for large cities over the course of the panel in these twenty-seven states.

41. https://www.citrusheights.net/197/Legislative-Advocacy.

42. For technical details, see Shor and McCarty (2011).

43. Interview with the author, March 11, 2021.

44. Even though the data indicate a weaker relationship between city mobilization and the partisan composition of the legislature, anecdotal evidence suggests that these dynamics do matter to the strategic decisions of city lobbyists. When I asked Milwaukee lobbyist Jennifer Abele whether she changed her approach based on the party in control of state government, she responded, "It absolutely changed our approach. Everything starts with the state budget. When we knew [Democratic governor Jim Doyle] was starting his conversation with his team about what he was going to propose for the state budget, we met with all the cabinet people in the state budget office to go through our legislative package. We tried to get as much as possible into the budget during the proposal phase. We tended to work more actively with the administration on the budget proposal when there was a Democratic governor." (Interview with the author, March 5, 2021.)

45. Interview with the author, May 11, 2018.

Chapter 4

1. https://www.auditor.leg.state.mn.us/ped/1990/90-02.pdf.

2. For precise numbers on the proportion of cities lobbying across states, see Table A2.1 in the Chapter 2 appendix.

3. See Chapter 2 for a detailed discussion of the construction of the dataset.

4. Other states passed their tax and expenditure limitations in the 1980s and 1990s (Kousser, McCubbins, and Moule 2008).

5. Walczak (2018).

6. Interview with the author, April 8, 2021.

7. Interview with the author, March 4, 2021.

8. Wilson (2015).

9. Baeder (2014).

10. Interview with the author, Sept. 19, 2017.

11. Spector (2014).

12. Harrie (2015).

13. See Table A4.1 in the chapter appendix.

14. Maciag (2016).

15. *Crawford v. Imperial Irrigation Dist.*, 200 Cal. 318, 324–25 (1927).

16. Stevens (2007).

17. Americans for Prosperity (2007), "Harris County Commissioners Rebuke Taxpayer-Funded Lobbying," https://web.archive.org/web/20090316040510/http://www.americansfor prosperity.org/harris-county-takes-unprecedented-step-pulling-out-texas-association-counties.

18. Auslen and Bousquet (2017).

19. Shumway (2017).

20. Auslen and Bousquet (2017).

21. Drew (2017).

Chapter 5

1. Rosewicz, Biernacka-Lievestro, and Newman (2019).

2. Harrie (2015).

3. https://le.utah.gov/~2015/bills/static/HB0420.html.

4. Harrie (2015).

5. https://www.townsendpa.com/about-tpa/.

6. Interview with the author, April 8, 2021.

7. Myers (2015).

8. Rudoren and Pilhofer (2006).

9. Hevesi (2005), "Local Government Issues in Focus: Revenue Sharing in New York State," Office of the New York State Comptroller, https://www.osc.state.ny.us/localgov/pubs/research/rev_sharing.pdf.

10. Note that recent work by Anzia argues that one of the reasons why research on interest groups has struggled to document influence is because of the literature's near-exclusive focus on federal politics and policy. In the subnational context, the power of interest groups is often more visible and easier to detect. See Anzia (2019).

11. Nidever (2015).

12. For additional details on the construction of the dataset, see Chapter 2.

13. The California data span the years 2002–2015, Washington from 2007 to 2015, and Florida from 2009 to 2015.

14. Results look similar but a bit noisier when using log total transfers as an outcome. See Table A5.4 in the chapter appendix.

15. Results available in the online replication files.

16. Harrie (2015).

17. Doughman (2013).

18. Finke (2013).

19. Herz (2016).
20. Klopsch (2018).
21. Interview with the author, April 8, 2021.
22. Specifically, I interact the lobbying indicator with a city's logged median income, using the same difference-in-differences approach introduced in the previous section. I also bin cities into income levels to address the potential problems raised by continuous moderators in Hainmueller, Mummolo, and Xu (2019). The results are virtually identical.
23. Interview with the author, September 20, 2017.
24. The data on the bills being lobbied come from https://www.sos.ca.gov/campaign-lobbying/cal-access-resources/raw-data-campaign-finance-and-lobbying-activity. I match mentions of bills with their subject matter described at the California State Legislature website:https://leginfo.legislature.ca.gov/faces/billSearchClient.xhtml. I focus specifically on bills introduced in the assembly (ABs) or senate (SBs), rather than on special legislation.
25. Interestingly, high-income cities were no more likely to mention lobbying for grants compared to low-income cities in their lobbying disclosure reports. This doesn't mean that affluent cities weren't applying for grants, but it does suggest that they weren't disproportionately hiring lobbyists to craft their application.
26. Interview with the author, March 4, 2021.

Chapter 6

1. Stokes and Sivasailam (2012).
2. Center on Budget and Policy Priorities (2018), "Policy Basics: Where Do Our State Tax Dollars Go?" http://www.cbpp.org/research/state-budget-and-tax/policy-basics-where-do-our-state-tax- dollars-go.
3. These models also include state and year fixed effects that confine the analysis to within-state comparisons.
4. Rove (2010).
5. Parker et al. (2018).
6. See Hertel-Fernandez (2019) for more on the rise of ALEC and other conservative business interests.
7. https://www.alec.org/model-policy/living-wage-mandate-preemption-act/.
8. Huizar (2019b).
9. Iannelli (2019).
10. WUFT (2018), "Gainesville among 10 Cities Joining a Legal Challenge of Gun Law Penalties," May 16, https://www.wuft.org/news/2018/05/16/gainesville-among-10-cities-joining-a-legal-challenge-of-gun-law-penalties/.
11. Cournoyer (2018).
12. Interview with the author, March 11, 2021.
13. Huizar (2019a).

14. https://www.sos.state.co.us/lobby/SearchSubject.do.
15. City of Rockville (2018), "Request for Proposal 06-19: State Lobbying and Legislative Representation Services," https://www.rockvillemd.gov/DocumentCenter/View/28369/RFP-06-19-State-Lobbying-and-Legislative-Representation-Services?bidId=.
16. Connecticut General Assembly website: https://cga.ct.gov/asp/menu/CommDocTmy.asp?comm_code=ph&date=03/20/2017.
17. Bean and Strano (2019).
18. Herz (2016).
19. See, for example, the position papers posted by the Colorado Municipal League at https://www.cml.org/home/advocacy-legal/position-papers.
20. Kinney (2017).
21. Interview with the author, March 4, 2021.
22. Local Solutions Support Center website: https://www.supportdemocracy.org/mission.
23. Nicol (2019).
24. A Better Balance (2017), "Legal Strategies to Counter State Preemption and Protect Progressive Localism: A Summary of the Findings of the Legal Effort to Address Preemption (LEAP) Project," August 9, https://www.abetterbalance.org/resources/legal-strategies-to-counter-state-preemption-and-protect-progressive-localism-a-summary-of-the-findings-of-the- legal-effort-to-address-preemption-leap-project/.
25. A Better Balance (2017), "Legal Strategies to Counter State Preemption and Protect Progressive Localism: A Summary of the Findings of the Legal Effort to Address Preemption (LEAP) Project," August 9, https://www.abetterbalance.org/resources/legal-strategies-to-counter-state-preemption-and-protect-progressive-localism-a-summary-of-the-findings-of-the-legal-effort-to-address-preemption-leap-project/.
26. Spector (2016).
27. Baeder (2014).

Chapter 7

1. Spector (2016).
2. Coolican (2016).
3. Kerpen (2007).
4. Carlson (2017).
5. Auslen and Bousquet (2017).
6. Simon (2009).
7. Bean and Strano (2019).
8. Schrader (2015); Texas Public Policy Foundation (2019), "Coalition Demands Eliminating Taxpayer-Funded Lobbying," March 13, https://www.texaspolicy.com/press/coalition-demands-eliminating-taxpayer-funded-lobbying.
9. Drew (2017).
10. Maciag (2016).

11. Baeder (2014).
12. Harrie (2015).
13. Fonger (2009).
14. Peterson (2005).
15. Coolican (2016).
16. Humphrey (2014).
17. Linehan (2016).
18. Interview with the author, September 26, 2017.
19. See, for example, State of Minnesota, Office of the State Auditor (2017), "2016 Local Government Lobbying Services," https://www.leg.mn.gov/docs/2017/mandated/170665.pdf.

Chapter 2 Appendix

1. https://www.ncsl.org/research/ethics/50-state-chart-lobby-definitions.aspx and https://www.ncsl.org/research/ethics/50-state-chart-lobbyist-report-requirements.aspx.

Bibliography

Alesina, Alberto, Reza Baqir, and William Easterly. 1999. "Public Goods and Ethnic Divisions." *The Quarterly Journal of Economics* 114(4): 1243–1284.

Alexander, Raquel Meyer, Stephen W. Mazza, and Susan Scholz. 2009. "Measuring Rates of Return for Lobbying Expenditures: An Empirical Case Study of Tax Breaks for Multinational Corporations." *Journal of Law & Politics* 25(4): 401–458.

Allard, Scott, Nancy Burns, and Gerald Gamm. 1998. "Representing Urban Interests: The Local Politics of State Legislatures." *Studies in American Political Development* 12(2): 267–302.

Angrist, Joshua D., and Jörn-Steffen Pischke. 2008. *Mostly Harmless Econometrics: An Empiricist's Companion*. Princeton, NJ: Princeton University Press.

Ansolabehere, Stephen, and James M. Snyder. 2008. *The End of Inequality: One Person, One Vote and the Transformation of American Politics*. New York: W. W. Norton.

Ansolabehere, Stephen, John M. De Figueiredo, and James M. Snyder. 2003. "Why Is There So Little Money in U.S. Politics?" *Journal of Economic Perspectives* 17(1): 105–130.

Anzia, Sarah F. 2019. "Looking for Influence in All the Wrong Places: How Studying Subnational Policy Can Revive Research on Interest Groups." *Journal of Politics* 81(1): 343–351.

Auslen, Michael, and Steve Bousquet. 2017. "Taxpayers Will Keep Paying for Lobbyists in Tallahassee, despite House Speaker, Who Calls It a 'Disgrace.'" *Tampa Bay Times*, Jan 7, https://www.tampabay.com/news/politics/legislature/house-speaker-richard-corcoran-takes-aim-at-government-paid-lobbying/2308603/.

Austen-Smith, David. 1993. "Information and Influence: Lobbying for Agendas and Votes." *American Journal of Political Science* 37(3): 799–833.

Baeder, Ben. 2014. "Who Pays the Most for California Government Lobbying in Sacramento? Government." *Los Angeles Daily News*, July 6, https://www.dailynews.com/2014/07/06/who-pays-the-most-for-california-government-lobbying-in-sacramento-government/.

Barber, Michael J. 2016. "Ideological Donors, Contribution Limits, and the Polarization of American Legislatures." *Journal of Politics* 78(1): 296–310.

Bartels, Larry. 2008. *Unequal Democracy: The Political Economy of the New Gilded Age*. Princeton, NJ: Princeton University Press.

Bauer, Raymond A., Ithiel de Sola Pool, and Lewis Anthony Dexter. 1963. *American Business & Public Policy*. Chicago: Atherton Press.

Baumgartner, Frank R., Jeffrey M. Berry, Marie Hojnacki, David C. Kimball, and Beth L. Leech. 2012. *Lobbying and Policy Change: Who Wins, Who Loses, and Why*. Chicago: University of Chicago Press.

Baumgartner, Frank R., and Beth L. Leech. 1998. *Basic Interests: The Importance of Groups in Politics and in Political Science*. Princeton, NJ: Princeton University Press.

Bean, Lydia, and Maresa Strano. 2019. "Punching Down: How States Are Suppressing Local Democracy." *New America*, December 21, https://www.newamerica.org/political-reform/reports/punching-down/.

Beard, Charles Austin. 1913. *American City Government: A Survey of Newer Tendencies*. London: WCTF Unwin.

Berkman, Michael B. 2001. "Legislative Professionalism and the Demand for Groups: The Institutional Context of Interest Population Density." *Legislative Studies Quarterly* 26(4): 661–679.

Berman, David R. 2003. *Local Government and the States: Autonomy, Politics, and Policy*. New York: M. E. Sharpe.

Berry, Christopher R. 2009. *Imperfect Union: Representation and Taxation in Multilevel Governments*. Cambridge, UK: Cambridge University Press.

Bertrand, Marianne, Matilde Bombardini, and Franceso Trebbi. 2014. "Is It Whom You Know or What You Know? An Empirical Assessment of the Lobbying Process." *American Economic Review* 104(12): 3885–3920.

Blanes i Vidal, Jordi, Mirko Draca, and Christian Fons-Rosen. 2012. "Revolving Door Lobbyists." *American Economic Review* 102(7): 3731–3748.

Bowling, Cynthia J., and Margaret R. Ferguson. 2001. "Divided Government, Interest Representation, and Policy Differences: Competing Explanations of Gridlock in the Fifty States." *Journal of Politics* 63(1): 182–206.

Brenan, Megan. 2017. "Nurses Keep Healthy Lead as Most Honest, Ethical Profession." *Gallup.com*, December 26, https://news.gallup.com/poll/224639/nurses-keep-healthy-lead-honest-ethical-profession.aspx.

Britschgi, Christian. 2017. "Local Governments Spend Big on Lobbyists." *Reason*, August 8, https://reason.com/2017/08/08/local-governments-spend-big-on-lobbyists/.

Brollo, Fernanda, and Tommaso Nannicini. 2012. "Tying Your Enemy's Hands in Close Races: The Politics of Federal Transfers in Brazil." *American Political Science Review* 106(4): 742–761.

Burns, Nancy, Laura Evans, Gerald Gamm, and Corrine McConnaughy. 2009. "Urban Politics in the State Arena." *Studies in American Political Development* 23(1): 1.

Burns, Nancy, and Gerald Gamm. 1997. "Creatures of the State: State Politics and Local Government, 1871–1921." *Urban Affairs Review* 33(1): 59–96.

Cain, Bruce, and Thad Kousser. 2004. *Adapting to Term Limits: Recent Experiences and New Directions*. San Francisco: Public Policy Institute of California.

Cain, Bruce, and Marc A. Levin. 1999. "Term Limits." *Annual Review of Political Science* 2: 163–188.

Cammisa, Anne M. 1995. *Governments as Interest Groups: Intergovernmental Lobbying and the Federal System*. Westport, CT: Praeger.

Carey, John M., Richard G. Niemi, and Lynda W. Powell. 2000. *Term Limits in the State Legislatures*. Ann Arbor: University of Michigan Press.

Carlson, Heather J. 2017. "Minnesota Taxpayer Funded Lobbying." *Northern Plains News*, April 27, http://northernplainsnews.com/articles/minnesotalobbying.php.

Caughey, Devin, and Christopher Warshaw. 2016. "The Dynamics of State Policy Liberalism, 1936–2014." *American Journal of Political Science* 60(4): 899–913.

Chen, Jowei. 2010. "The Effect of Electoral Geography on Pork Barreling in Bicameral Legislatures." *American Journal of Political Science* 54(2): 301–322.

Cigler, Beverly A. 1995. "Not Just Another Special Interest: Intergovernmental Representation." *Interest Group Politics* 4: 131–153.

Cigler, Beverly A. 2012. "Not Just Another Special Interest: The Intergovernmental Lobby Revisited." In *Interest Group Politics*, 8th ed., edited by Allan J. Cigler and Burdett A. Loomis, 264–296. Washington, DC: CQ Press.

Clarke, Wes. 1998. "Divided Government and Budget Conflict in the US States." *Legislative Studies Quarterly* 23(1): 5–22.

Conlan, Tim. 2006. "From Cooperative to Opportunistic Federalism: Reflections on the Half-Century Anniversary of the Commission on Intergovernmental Relations." *Public Administration Review* 66(5): 663–676.

Coolican, Patrick J. 2016. "Governments Spend Millions Lobbying Government." *Star Tribune*, March 28, https://www.startribune.com/governments-spend-millions-lobbying-government/373685161/.

Cournoyer, Caroline. 2018. "With No Power to Pass Gun Laws, Florida Cities Prepare Plan B (and C)." *Governing*, March 20, https://www.governing.com/archive/gov-florida-weston- miami-gun-coral-springs-cables-gun-nra.html.

Craver, Jack. 2019. "Exit Eckstein: Travis County's Retiring Lobbyist Reflects on His Battles at the Legislature." *Austin Monitor*, November 18, https://www.austinmonitor.com/stories/2019/11/exit-eckstein-travis-countys-retiring-lobbyist- reflects-on-his-battles-at-the-legislature/.

Dahl, Robert A. 1961. *Who Governs? Democracy and Power in an American City*. New Haven: Yale University Press.

Danielson, Michael N., and Paul G. Lewis. 1996. "City Bound: Political Science and the American Metropolis." *Political Research Quarterly* 49(1): 203–220.

De Benedictis-Kessner, Justin. 2018. "Off-Cycle and Out of Office: Election Timing and the Incumbency Advantage." *Journal of Politics* 80(1): 119–132.

De Benedictis-Kessner, Justin, and Christopher Warshaw. 2016. "Mayoral Partisanship and Municipal Fiscal Policy." *Journal of Politics* 78(4): 1124–1138.

De Chaisemartin, Clément, and Xavier d'Haultfoeuille. 2018. "Fuzzy Differences-in-Differences." *Review of Economic Studies* 85(2): 999–1028.

De Figueiredo, John M., and Brian K. Richter. 2014. "Advancing the Empirical Research on Lobbying." *Annual Review of Political Science* 17: 163–185.

De Figueiredo, John M., and Brian S. Silverman. 2006. "Academic Earmarks and the Returns to Lobbying." *Journal of Law and Economics* 49(2): 597–625.

deMarrais, Kathleen, T. Jameson Brewer, Jamie C. Atkinson, Brigette A. Herron, and Jamie B. Lewis. 2019. *Philanthropy, Hidden Strategy, and Collective Resistance: A Primer for Concerned Educators*. Gorham, ME: Myers Education Press.

Denzau, Arthur T., and Michael C. Munger. 1986. "Legislators and Interest Groups: How Unorganized Interests Get Represented." *American Political Science Review* 80(1): 89–106.

De Soto, William. 1995. "Cities in State Politics: Views of Mayors and Managers." *State and Local Government Review* 27(3): 188–194.

Doughman, Andrew. 2013. "Taxpayers Footing $3 Million Lobbying Bill for Local Governments." *Las Vegas Sun*, May 10, https://lasvegassun.com/news/2013/may/10/taxpayers-footing-3-million-lobbying-bill-local-go/.

Drew, James. 2017. "Debate Intensifies over Texas Cities Using Taxpayer Dollars to Lobby." *Houston Chronicle*, August 22, https://www.houstonchronicle.com/news/politics/texas/article/Debate-intensifies-over-Texas-cities-using-tax-11951361.php.

Drope, Jeffrey M., and Wendy L. Hansen. 2006. "Does Firm Size Matter? Analyzing Business Lobbying in the United States." *Business and Politics* 8(32): 1–17.

Drutman, Lee. 2015. *The Business of America Is Lobbying*. Oxford: Oxford University Press.

DuPuis, Nicole, Trevor Langan, Christiana McFarland, Angelina Panettieri, and Brooks Rainwater. 2018. "City Rights in an Era of Preemption: A State-by-State Analysis." *The National League of Cities*, https://www.nlc.org/resource/city-rights-in-an-era-of-preemption-a-state-by-state-analysis/.

Einstein, Katherine Levine, and David M. Glick. 2017. "Cities in American Federalism: Evidence on State–Local Government Conflict from a Survey of Mayors." *Publius: The Journal of Federalism* 47(4): 599–621.

Einstein, Katherine Levine, and Vladimir Kogan. 2016. "Pushing the City Limits: Policy Responsiveness in Municipal Government." *Urban Affairs Review* 52(1): 3–32.

Farkas, Suzanne. 1971. *Urban Lobbying: Mayors in the Federal Arena*. New York: New York University Press.

Fernandes, Alan N. 2009. "Ethical Considerations of the Public Sector Lobbyist." *McGeorge Law Review* 41(1): 183–202.

Finch, Roy G. 1925. "The Story of the New York State Canals." Albany: State Engineer and Surveyor, https://www.canals.ny.gov/history/finch_history.pdf.

Finke, Doug. 2013. "Local Governments Split on Hiring Lobbyists." *State Journal Register*, August 11, https://www.sj-r.com/article/20130811/news/308119958?template=ampart.

Flanagan, Richard M. 1999. "Roosevelt, Mayors and the New Deal Regime: The Origins of Intergovernmental Lobbying and Administration." *Polity* 31(3): 415–450.

Flavin, Patrick. 2014. "State Campaign Finance Laws and the Equality of Political Representation." *Election Law Journal* 13(3): 362–374.

Fonger, Ron. 2009. "Taxpayers Pay When Local Government Agencies Play Politics." *Michigan Live*, May 10, https://www.mlive.com/news/flint/2009/12/taxpayers_pay_when_local_gover.html.

Freeman, Patricia K., and Anthony J. Nownes. 1999. "Intergovernmental Lobbying in the States." *Politics and Policy* 27(4): 619–634.

Freer, Emma. 2019. "Travis County Commissioners Push Back against Proposed Rollback Tax Rate, Advocate for School Finance Reform." *Community Impact Newspaper*, February 20, https://communityimpact.com/austin/central-austin/city-county/2019/02/20/travis-county-commissioners-push-back-against-proposed-rollback-tax-rate-advocate-for-school-finance-reform/.

Gamm, Gerald, and Thad Kousser. 2010. "Broad Bills or Particularistic Policy? Historical Patterns in American State Legislatures." *American Political Science Review* 104(1): 151–170.

Gamm, Gerald, and Thad Kousser. 2013. "No Strength in Numbers: The Failure of Big-City Bills in American State Legislatures, 1880–2000." *American Political Science Review* 107(4): 663–678.

Gerber, Elisabeth R., and Daniel J. Hopkins. 2011. "When Mayors Matter: Estimating the Impact of Mayoral Partisanship on City Policy." *American Journal of Political Science* 55(2): 326–339.

Gilens, Martin. 2012. *Affluence and Influence: Economic Inequality and Political Power in America*. Princeton, NJ: Princeton University Press.

Gilens, Martin, and Benjamin I. Page. 2014. "Testing Theories of American Politics: Elites, Interest Groups, and Average Citizens." *Perspectives on Politics* 12(3): 564–581.

Goldstein, Rebecca, and Hye Young You. 2017. "Cities as Lobbyists." *American Journal of Political Science* 61(4): 864–876.

Gonsalves, Joe A. 2002. *A Capital Life*. Sacramento, CA: Carvell Printing.

Goodman-Bacon, Andrew. 2018. "Difference-in-Differences with Variation in Treatment Timing." Working Paper Series 25018. Cambridge, MA: National Bureau of Economic Research.

Goodrich, Carter. 1960. *Government Promotion of American Canals and Railroads, 1800–1890*. New York: Columbia University Press.

Gordon, Sanford C., and Catherine Hafer. 2005. "Flexing Muscle: Corporate Political Expenditures as Signals to the Bureaucracy." *American Political Science Review* 99(2): 245–261.

Gray, Virginia, John Cluverius, Jeffrey J. Harden, Boris Shor, and David Lowery. 2015. "Party Competition, Party Polarization, and the Changing Demand for Lobbying in the American States." *American Politics Research* 43(2): 175–204.

Gray, Virginia, and David Lowery. 1996. *The Population Ecology of Interest Representation: Lobbying Communities in the American States*. Ann Arbor: University of Michigan Press.

Grenzke, Janet M. 1989. "PACs and the Congressional Supermarket: The Currency Is Complex." *American Journal of Political Science* 33(1): 1–24.

Grier, Kevin B., Michael C. Munger, and Brian E. Roberts. 1994. "The Determinants of Industry Political Activity, 1978–1986." *American Political Science Review* 88(4): 911–926.

Grossman, Gene M., and Elhanan Helpman. 2001. *Special Interest Politics*. Cambridge, MA: MIT Press.

Grossmann, Matt. 2013. *New Directions in Interest Group Politics*. New York: Routledge.

Haider, Donald H. 1974. *When Governments Come to Washington: Governors, Mayors, and Intergovernmental Lobbying*. New York: The Free Press.

Hainmueller, Jens, Jonathan Mummolo, and Yiqing Xu. 2019. "How Much Should We Trust Estimates from Multiplicative Interaction Models? Simple Tools to Improve Empirical Practice." *Political Analysis* 27(2): 163–192.

Hajnal, Zoltan, and Jessica Trounstine. 2005. "Where Turnout Matters: The Consequences of Uneven Turnout in City Politics." *Journal of Politics* 67(2): 515–535.

Hall, Richard L., and Alan V. Deardorff. 2006. "Lobbying as Legislative Subsidy." *American Political Science Review* 100(1): 69–84.

Hall, Richard L., and Frank W. Wayman. 1990. "Buying Time: Moneyed Interests and the Mobilization of Bias in Congressional Committees." *American Political Science Review* 84(3): 797–820.

Hansen, Wendy L., and Neil J. Mitchell. 2001. "Globalization or National Capitalism: Large Firms, National Strategies, and Political Activities." *Business and Politics* 3(1): 5–19.

Harden, Jeffrey J. 2013. "Multidimensional Responsiveness: The Determinants of Legislators' Representational Priorities." *Legislative Studies Quarterly* 38(2): 155–184.

Harrie, Dan. 2015. "Utah Cities Turning to Lobbyists as Their Lifeline to the Legislature." *Salt Lake Tribune*, July 12, https://archive.sltrib.com/article.php?id=2714828&itype=CMSID.

Hart, David M. 2001. "Why Do Some Firms Give? Why Do Some Give a Lot? High-Tech PACs, 1977–1996." *Journal of Politics* 63(4): 1230–1249.

Hertel-Fernandez, Alexander. 2019. *State Capture: How Conservative Activists, Big Businesses, and Wealthy Donors Reshaped the American States—and the Nation*. New York: Oxford University Press.

Herz, Nathaniel. 2016. "Local Interests Paying More for Lobbyists at Cash-Strapped Alaska Capitol." *Anchorage Daily News*, February 14, https://www.adn.com/politics/article/alaska-communities-school-districts-paying-more-lobbyists-cash-strapped-capitol/2016/02/15/.

Hillman, Amy J., Gerald D. Keim, and Douglas Schuler. 2004. "Corporate Political Activity: A Review and Research Agenda." *Journal of Management* 30(6): 837–857.

Hojnacki, Marie, David C. Kimball, Frank R. Baumgartner, Jeffrey M. Berry, and Beth L. Leech. 2012. "Studying Organizational Advocacy and Influence: Reexamining Interest Group Research." *Annual Review of Political Science* 15: 379–399.

Hopkins, Daniel J. 2009. "The Diversity Discount: When Increasing Ethnic and Racial Diversity Prevents Tax Increases." *Journal of Politics* 71(1): 160–177.

Hrebenar, Ronald J., and Bryson B. Morgan. 2009. *Lobbying in America: A Reference Handbook*. Santa Barbara, CA: ABC-CLIO.

Hrebener, Ronald J., and Clive S. Thomas. 1987. *Interest Group Politics in the American West*. Salt Lake City: University of Utah Press.

Hrebenar, Ronald J., and Clive S. Thomas. 1993a. *Interest Group Politics in the Midwestern States*. Ames: Iowa State University Press.

Hrebenar, Ronald J., and Clive S. Thomas. 1993b. *Interest Group Politics in the Northeastern States*. University Park: Pennsylvania State University Press.

Huizar, Laura. 2019a. "Colorado Should Approve HB 19-1210 to Protect Local Democracy and Support Workers in High Cost-of-Living Areas." *National Employment Law Project*, March 6, https://www.nelp.org/publication/colorado-should-approve-hb-19-1210-to-protect-local-   democracy-and-support-workers-in-high-cost-of-living-areas/.

Huizar, Laura. 2019b. "Maryland Legislators Should Protect Local Democracy and Say No to Preemption of Local Minimum Wage Laws." *National Employment Law Project*, March 5, https://www.nelp.org/publication/maryland-legislators-protect-local-democracy-say-no-preemption-local-minimum-wage-laws/#_edn17.

Humphrey, Tom. 2014. "Governments Hire Lobbyists to Lobby . . . Government." *The Tennessean*, January 9, https://www.tennessean.com/story/news/politics/2014/01/10/governments-hire-lobbyists-to-lobby-government/4399855/.

Iannelli, Jerry. 2019. "Florida Republicans Are Going to War against Small Government." *Miami New Times*, May 12, https://www.miaminewtimes.com/news/florida-republican-preemption-laws-in-2019-legislative-session-fight-against-small-government-11169504.

Inman, Robert P., and Daniel L. Rubinfeld. 1997. "Rethinking Federalism." *Journal of Economic Perspectives* 11(4): 43–64.

Jensen, Jennifer M. 2019. "Intergovernmental Lobbying in the United States: Assessing the Benefits of Accumulated Knowledge." *State and Local Government Review* 50(4): 270–281.

Jewell, Malcolm E. 1982. *Representation in State Legislatures*. Lexington: University Press of Kentucky.

Jordan, Marty P., and Matt Grossmann. 2020. "The Correlates of State Policy Project v.2.1." East Lansing, MI: Institute for Public Policy and Social Research.

Judd, Dennis, and Todd Swanstrom. 2015. *City Politics*. London and New York: Routledge.

KCET. 2011. "How Democrats Fooled California's Redistricting Commission." *KCET.org*, December 21, https://www.kcet.org/socal-focus/how-democrats-fooled-californias-redistricting-commission.

Kerpen, Phil. 2007. "Taxpayer-Funded Lobbying Fuels Big Government." *National Review*, May 24, https://www.nationalreview.com/2007/05/taxpayer-funded-lobbying-fuels-big-government-phil-kerpen/.

Kinney, Jen. 2017. "When Red Statehouses Overrule Blue City Halls." *Next City*, February 24, https://nextcity.org/daily/entry/when-red-statehouses-overrule-blue-city-halls-preemtive-laws.

Klopsch, Jana. 2018. "Taylorsville Contracts with a Lobbyist to Tout City among State Lawmakers." *Taylorsville City Journal*, October 5, https://www.taylorsvillecityjournal.com/2018/10/05/181576/taylorsville-contracts-with-a- lobbyist-to- tout-city-among-state-lawmakers.

Kousser, Thad, Mathew D. McCubbins, and Ellen Moule. 2008. "For Whom the TEL Tolls: Can State Tax and Expenditure Limits Effectively Reduce Spending?" *State Politics and Policy Quarterly* 8(4): 331–361.

LaPira, Timothy M., and Herschel F. Thomas. 2017. *Revolving Door Lobbying: Public Service, Private Influence, and the Unequal Representation of Interests*. Lawrence: University Press of Kansas.

Lax, Jeffrey R., and Justin H. Phillips. 2009. "Gay Rights in the States: Public Opinion and Policy Responsiveness." *American Political Science Review* 103(3): 367–386.

Lazarus, Jeffrey. 2009. "Party, Electoral Vulnerability, and Earmarks in the US House of Representatives." *Journal of Politics* 71(3): 1050–1061.

Levitt, Steven D., and James M. Snyder. 1997. "The Impact of Federal Spending on House Election Outcomes." *Journal of Political Economy* 105(1): 30–53.

Linehan, Dan. 2016. "Government Pays Millions to Watch Government." *Mankato Free Press*, April 2, https://www.mankatofreepress.com/news/government-pays-millions-to-watch- government/article_906334c2-f556-11e5-a233-17d084dab669.html.

Liu, Licheng, Ye Wang, and Yiqing Xu. 2020. "A Practical Guide to Counterfactual Estimators for Causal Inference with Time-Series Cross-Sectional Data." Available at SSRN: ,https://dx.doi.org/10.2139/ssrn.3555463.

Loftis, Matt W., and Jaclyn J. Kettler. 2015. "Lobbying from Inside the System: Why Local Governments Pay for Representation in the US Congress." *Political Research Quarterly* 68(1): 193–206.

Longley, Kristin. 2011. "Flint's Bishop Airport Lands $3.3 Million Grant for Expansion." *Michigan Live*, August 30, https://www.mlive.com/news/flint/2011/08/flints_bishop_airport_lands_33.html.

Lowery, David. 2007. "Why Do Organized Interests Lobby? A Multi-Goal, Multi-Context Theory of Lobbying." *Polity* 39(1): 29–54.

Lowery, David, and Holly Brasher. 2004. *Organized Interests and American Government*. New York: McGraw-Hill.

Lowery, David, Virginia Gray, John Cluverius, and Jeffrey J. Harden. 2012. "Explaining the Anomalous Growth of Public Sector Lobbying in the American States, 1997–2007." *Publius: The Journal of Federalism* 43(4): 580–599.

Lowi, Theodore. 1969. *The End of Liberalism*. New York: W. W. Norton.

Maciag, Mike. 2016. "Gov2Gov: The Lobbying That Falls under the Radar." *Governing*, June 27, https://www.governing.com/archive/gov-federal-lobbying-spending.html.

Maestas, Cherie. 2000. "Professional Legislatures and Ambitious Politicians: Policy Responsiveness of State Institutions." *Legislative Studies Quarterly* 25(4): 663–690.

Marin, Max. 2017. "Kenney Hiring lobbyists to Buddy Up with GOP Leadership." *City and State Pennsylvania*, April 14, https://www.cityandstatepa.com/content/kenney-hiring-lobbyists-buddy-gop-leadership.

Marschall, Melissa J. 2010. "The Study of Local Elections in American Politics." In *The Oxford Handbook of American Elections and Political Behavior*, edited by Jan E. Leighley, 471–492. New York: Oxford University Press.

McGreevy, Patrick, and Phil Willon. 2015. "State Lawmakers Request Millions in Funding for District Projects." *Los Angeles Times*, June 12, https://www.latimes.com/local/politics/la-me-pol-budget-earmarks-20150613-story.html.

Milbrath, Lester W. 1963. *The Washington Lobbyists*. Chicago: Rand McNally.

Mills, C. Wright. 1956. *The Power Elite*. New York: Oxford University Press.

Mitchell, Neil J., Wendy L. Hansen, and Eric M. Jepsen. 1997. "The Determinants of Domestic and Foreign Corporate Political Activity." *Journal of Politics* 59(4): 1096–1113.

Mitchell, William C., and Michael C. Munger. 1991. "Economic Models of Interest Groups: An Introductory Survey." *American Journal of Political Science* 35(2): 512–546.

Moncrief, Gary, and Joel A. Thompson. 2001. "On the Outside Looking In: Lobbyists' Perspectives on the Effects of State Legislative Term Limits." *State Politics and Policy Quarterly* 1(4): 394–411.

Morgan, David. 1984. "Use of Public Funds for Legislative Lobbying and Electoral Campaigning, The." *Vanderbilt Law Review* 37: 433.

Musgrave, Robert A. 1959. *The Theory of Public Finance*. New York: McGraw-Hill.

Myers, John. 2015. "Local Governments Spend Big to Influence Sacramento." *KQED.org*, August 12, https://www.kqed.org/news/10637900/local-governments-spend-big-to-influence-sacramento.

Nice, David C. 1987. *Federalism: The Politics of Intergovernmental Relations*. New York: St. Martin's Press.

Nicol, Ryan. 2019. "Poll from Anti-Preemption Group Shows Floridians Support Local Control." *Florida Politics*, November 6, https://floridapolitics.com/archives/310572-poll-floridians-support-local-control/.

Nidever, Seth. 2015. "Lemoore, Corcoran, Avenal Get $5 Million for Police Projects." *Hanford Sentinel*, June 26, https://hanfordsentinel.com/news/local/lemoore-corcoran-avenal-get-million-for-police-projects/article_59df1fa0-c52f-5b98-8d19-cd6e849c44c6.html.

Nownes, Anthony J. 2006. *Total Lobbying: What Lobbyists Want (and How They Try to Get It)*. Cambridge, UK: Cambridge University Press.

Nownes, Anthony J., and Patricia Freeman. 1998. "Interest Group Activity in the States." *Journal of Politics* 60(1): 86–112.

Oates, Wallace E. 1972. *Fiscal Federalism*. New York: Harcourt Brace Jovanovich.

Ogorzalek, Thomas K. 2018. *The Cities on the Hill: How Urban Institutions Transformed National Politics*. New York: Oxford University Press.

Olson, Mancur. 1965. *The Logic of Collective Action*. Cambridge, MA: Harvard University Press.

Parker, Kim, Juliana Menasce Horowitz, Anna Brown, Richard Fry, D'Vera Cohn, and Ruth Igielnik. 2018. "Urban, Suburban and Rural Residents' View on Key Social and Political Issues." *Pew Research Center*, May 22, https://www.pewresearch.org/social-trends/2018/05/22/urban-suburban-and-rural-residents-views-on-key-social-and-political-issues/.

Payson, Julia A. 2020a. "Cities in the Statehouse: How Local Governments Use Lobbyists to Secure State Funding." *Journal of Politics* 82(2): 403–417.

Payson, Julia A. 2020b. "The Partisan Logic of City Mobilization: Evidence from State Lobbying Disclosures." *American Political Science Review* 114(3): 1–14.

Perez, Arturo. 2008. "Earmarking State Taxes." The National Conference of State Legislatures, http://www.ncsl.org/documents/fiscal/earmarking-state-taxes.pdf.

Peterson, Paul. 1995. *The Price of Federalism*. Washington, DC: Brookings Institution Press.

Peterson, Paul E. 1981. *City Limits*. Chicago: University of Chicago Press.

Peterson, Rachel. 2005. "City Hires D.C. Lobbyist to Tap Pork Barrel." *Arizona Daily Sun*, September 11, https://azdailysun.com/city-hires-d-c-lobbyist-to-tap-pork- barrel/article_b7265b4a-2d77-5485-9ae3-4b57ceb21e4b.html.

Potters, Jan, and Frans Van Winden. 1992. "Lobbying and Asymmetric Information." *Public Choice* 74(3): 269–292.

Radelat, Ana. 2015. "State, Local Governments Hire Lobbyists for Influence in D.C." *CT Mirror*, January 15, https://ctmirror.org/2015/01/15/state-local-governments-hire-lobbyists-for-influence-in-d-c/.

Radnofsky, Louise, and Leslie Eaton. 2009. "States, Cities Spend for Stimulus Cash." *Wall Street Journal*, August 3, https://www.wsj.com/articles/SB124925597008100187.

Richter, Brian Kelleher, Krislert Samphantharak, and Jeffrey F. Timmons. 2009. "Lobbying and Taxes." *American Journal of Political Science* 53(4): 893–909.

Riverstone-Newell, Lori. 2017. "The Rise of State Preemption Laws in Response to Local Policy Innovation." *Publius: The Journal of Federalism* 47(3): 403–425.

Rodden, Jonathan A. 2019. *Why Cities Lose: The Deep Roots of the Urban-Rural Political Divide*. New York: Basic Books.

Rodríguez-Pose, Andrés, and Roberto Ezcurra. 2009. "Does Decentralization Matter for Regional Disparities? A Cross-Country Analysis." *Journal of Economic Geography* 10(5): 619–644.

Rosenthal, Alan. 1993. *The Third House: Lobbyists and Lobbying in the States*. Washington, DC: CQ Press.

Rosewicz, Barb, Joanna Biernacka-Lievestro, and Daniel Newman. 2019. "Western, Southern States Gain Residents the Fastest." *Pew Trust*, February 27, https://news.gallup.com/poll/224639/nurses-keep-healthy-lead-honest-ethical-profession.aspx.

Rove, Karl. 2010. "The GOP Targets State Legislatures." *Wall Street Journal*, March 4, https://www.wsj.com/articles/SB10001424052748703862704575099670689398044.

Rudoren, Jodi, and Aron Pilhofer. 2006. "Hiring Federal Lobbyists, Towns Learn Money Talks." *New York Times*, July 2, https://www.nytimes.com/2006/07/02/washington/02earmarks.html.

Salamon, Lester M., and John J. Siegfried. 1977. "Economic Power and Political Influence: The Impact of Industry Structure on Public Policy." *American Political Science Review* 71(3): 1026–1043.

Salisbury, Robert H. 1984. "Interest Representation: The Dominance of Institutions." *American Political Science Review* 78(1): 64–76.

Schattschneider, E. E. 1960. *The Semisovereign People*. New York: Holt, Rinehart and Winston.

Schlozman, Kay Lehman. 1984. "What Accent the Heavenly Chorus? Political Equality and the American Pressure System." *Journal of Politics* 46(4): 1006–1032.

Schlozman, Kay Lehman, and John T. Tierney. 1983. "More of the Same: Washington Pressure Group Activity in a Decade of Change." *Journal of Politics* 45(2): 351–377.

Schrader, Megan. 2015. "Is Lobbying of Politicians by Public Entities Government Waste or a Better Voice for Cities, Schools?" *Colorado Springs Gazette*, Sep 12, https://gazette.com/government/is-lobbying-of-politicians-by-public-entities-government-waste-or-a-better-voice-for-cities/article_770c429e-0acc-5e64-9cf7-2a4afcd62c4f.html.

Schragger, Richard C. 2017. "The Attack on American Cities." *Texas Law Review* 96: 1163.

Shor, Boris, and Nolan McCarty. 2011. "The Ideological Mapping of American Legislatures." *American Political Science Review* 105(3): 530–551.

Shor, Boris, and Nolan McCarty. 2015. "Individual State Legislator Shor-McCarty Ideology Data, June 2015 Update," https://doi.org/10.7910/DVN/THDBRA.

Shumway, Julia. 2017. "Nebraska Lawmakers Consider New Limits on Lobbyists." *AP News*, March 22, https://apnews.com/article/c130253dd3c24044ba4faa879539b5de.

Simon, Richard. 2009. "More Governments Look to Lobbyists." *Los Angeles Times*, September 27, https://www.latimes.com/archives/la-xpm-2009-sep-27-na-lobbying27-story.html.

Solé-Ollé, Albert, and Pilar Sorribas-Navarro. 2008. "The Effects of Partisan Alignment on the Allocation of Intergovernmental Transfers: Differences-in-Differences Estimates for Spain." *Journal of Public Economics* 92(12): 2302–2319.

Spector, Joseph. 2014. "Taxpayer Money Used to Pay Lobbyists." *The Journal News*, July 20, https://www.lohud.com/story/news/2014/07/20/new-york-lobbyists-monroe-county-nypirg/12918307/.

Spector, Joseph. 2016. "Armed with lobbyists, Yonkers Makes Final NY Aid Push." *The Journal News*, June 3, https://www.lohud.com/story/news/politics/politics-on-the-hudson/2016/06/03/armed-lobbyists-yonkers-makes-final-ny-aid-push/85342334/.

Squire, Peverill. 1992. "Legislative Professionalization and Membership Diversity in State Legislatures." *Legislative Studies Quarterly* 17(1): 69–79.

Squire, Peverill. 2007. "Measuring State Legislative Professionalism: The Squire Index Revisited." *State Politics and Policy Quarterly* 7(2): 211–227.

Stein, Robert M., and Kenneth N. Bickers. 1994. "Congressional Elections and the Pork Barrel." *Journal of Politics* 56(2): 377–399.

Stevens, Chris. 2007. "Tax Funded Lobby Groups Ruled Illegal (Americans for Prosperity vs. Texas Association of Counties)." *The Free Republic*, January 8, https://freerepublic.com/focus/f-news/1764243/posts.

Stigler, George J. 1971. "The Theory of Economic Regulation." *Bell Journal of Economics and Management Science* 2(1): 3–21.

Stokes, David, and Abhi Sivasailam. 2012. "Taxpayer-Funded Lobbying." *Show-Me Institute*, December, https://showmeinstitute.org/wp-content/uploads/2015/06/Essay_TaxpayerLobbyingFINAL120612_0.pdf.

Tausanovitch, Chris, and Christopher Warshaw. 2014. "Representation in Municipal Government." *American Political Science Review* 108(3): 605–641.

Teaford, Jon C. 1984. *The Unheralded Triumph: City Government in America, 1870–1900*. Baltimore: Johns Hopkins University Press.

Thomas, Clive S., and Ronald J Hrebenar. 2004. "Interest Groups in the States." In *Politics in the American States*, edited by Virginia Gray and Russell L. Hanson, 100–128. Washington, DC: CQ Press.

Tiebout, Charles M. 1956. "A Pure Theory of Local Expenditures." *Journal of Political Economy* 64(5): 416–424.

Tolbert, Caroline J., Karen Mossberger, and Ramona McNeal. 2008. "Institutions, Policy Innovation, and E-Government in the American States." *Public Administration Review* 68(3): 549–563.

Tripathi, Mickey. 2000. "PAC Contributions and Defense Contracting." *Business and Politics* 2(1): 53–73.

Trounstine, Jessica. 2016. "Segregation and Inequality in Public Goods." *American Journal of Political Science* 60(3): 709–725.

Truman, David B. 1951. *The Governmental Process: Public Interests and Public Opinion.* New York: Alfred A. Knopf.

Tullock, Gordon. 1967. "The Welfare Costs of Tariffs, Monopolies, and Theft." *Western Economic Journal* 5(3): 224–232.

Tullock, Gordon. 1972. "The Purchase of Politicians." *Western Economic Journal* 10: 354–355.

Verba, Sidney, Kay Lehman Schlozman, and Henry E. Brady. 1995. *Voice and Equality: Civic Voluntarism in American Politics.* Cambridge, MA: Harvard University Press.

Walczak, Jared. 2018. "Property Tax Limitation Regimes: A Primer." *Tax Foundation,* April 23, https://taxfoundation.org/property-tax-limitation-regimes-primer/.

Weir, Margaret. 1996. "Central Cities' Loss of Power in State Politics." *Cityscape* 2(2): 23–40.

Weir, Margaret, Harold Wolman, and Todd Swanstrom. 2005. "The Calculus of Coalitions: Cities, Suburbs, and the Metropolitan Agenda." *Urban Affairs Review* 40(6): 730–760.

Wilkinson, Will. 2019. "The Density Divide: Urbanization, Polarization, and Populist Backlash." Niskanen Center Research Paper. Washington, DC: Niskanen Center.

Wilson, Reid. 2015. "Amid Gridlock in D.C., Influence Industry Expands Rapidly in the States." *Washington Post,* May 11, https://www.washingtonpost.com/blogs/govbeat/wp/2015/05/11/amid-gridlock-in-d-c-influence-industry-expands-rapidly-in-the-states/.

Wright, John R. 1985. "PACs, Contributions, and Roll Calls: An Organizational Perspective." *American Political Science Review* 79(2): 400–414.

Wright, John R. 1990. "Contributions, Lobbying, and Committee Voting in the US House of Representatives." *American Political Science Review* 84(2): 417–438.

Zimmerman, Joseph F. 2012. *State-Local Governmental Interactions.* Albany: SUNY Press.

Index

For the benefit of digital users, indexed terms that span two pages (e.g., 52–53) may, on occasion, appear on only one of those pages.

Tables and figures are indicated by *t* and *f* following the page number